EQUITY RESEARCH for the TECHNOLC

By Sundeep Bajikar

Acknowledgements

This book is dedicated to my family and friends, who shaped the person that I have become.

On the family front, my mom, my mavshi (mom's sister), and dad went above and beyond to win me access to the best education and training I could have had growing up. They inculcated in me values of respect, trust, faith, kindness, and honesty, which have given me a resilient constitution, and helped me develop intuition and judgment. I trace my humility and determination back to my humble childhood upbringing, in an environment where I was provided opportunities to learn, many times in spite of adverse circumstances. The culture at home was forgiving enough that I was allowed to make mistakes and learn from them, but disciplined enough to make sure I stayed on track for academic success and a chance for higher education. I am grateful to my brother Nikhil for his support and faith in me.

My beautiful wife Kyunghee is one of the bravest and most determined people I know. Most of what I accomplished through a difficult career change from technology to finance would have been simply impossible without Kyunghee's dedicated and loving support. As we have learnt first-hand, it is not easy to keep a family together when the husband is continuously traveling for work, or is otherwise unavailable even if he is not traveling, because he is consumed by work. My five-year-old son Taeho's hugs and kisses have been the most potent stress relief that I have frequently and desperately needed. My hope is that this book will become a part of his financial education when he grows up.

I am grateful to my ex-colleague, mentor and friend Mark Lipacis, from whom I learnt a lot. He was always available as a selfless sounding board for my ideas, and to provide unlimited encouragement. Directors of Research Michael Eastwood (U.S.) and Nilesh Jasani (Asia) at Jefferies LLC, were kind enough to bless me with their faith, and trust me with progressively increasing coverage responsibilities – due to their generosity, I had the chance to cover a trillion dollars' worth of combined company market cap at Jefferies, and become the first analyst to cover the largest technology stocks in the U.S. (Apple) and Asia (Samsung Electronics) concurrently.

I am also grateful to the equity sales force at Jefferies, for putting their reputations on the line to get me in front of their best clients around the world. I was fortunate enough to have had the chance to routinely discuss and debate my views with investors across the U.S., U.K., Europe, Japan, Hong Kong, Singapore, South Korea, and Malaysia. I would like to thank Hong Kong based Global TMT Sales Specialist Conor O'Mara, and New York based desk analyst Justin Martos of Jefferies for their friendship, guidance, and help. I would also like to thank a number of equity sales team members at Jefferies, including – Brian Meringolo, Michael Cooley, Matt Mesa, Thomas Rossman, Tara Cone, Natti Ginor, Drew Mastromonaco, Dan Stratemeier, Rose Lee, James Young, Marcus Okuno, Jim Muir, Andy Winton, Caitlin Hart, Stephanie Muntner, Aroon Balani, Perry Jung, Balaji Jayaraman, Rachel An, Emery McConnell, Neil Higgins, Shanelle Trinidad, Scott Irving, John Mitchell, Tara Belisle, Ed Bonsor, Jade O'Brien, Bruce Ingram, Matt Brown, Hugo Sellers, Walid Armaly, Dan Furstenberg and Tom Egan.

I treasure my relationships with company managements, and buyside investors, both of which have been my clients, who put their faith in me to analyze available information with intelligence and integrity, and make investment recommendations that I would feel comfortable defending to anyone who cared to ask. I have been privileged also to be at the receiving end of feedback and training from experts in various disciplines within the tech industry – an opportunity that I could not even have dreamt of.

I am deeply grateful to my long-time friends Sameer Pardhy, Vivek Ganotra, Makarand Shinde, Gautam Sampath, Aidan Collins, Sanjay Verma, Shantanu Mitra, Rahul Limaye, Ashish Karandikar, Ketan Paranjape, Amit Baid, Raghu Raman, Rory McInerney, Bill Lu, Reuben Gallegos and Zack Perry for their reviews, encouragement and continuous guidance in writing this book.

I would like to extend special thanks to Jonathan Cheng of the Wall Street Journal (Seoul, South Korea Bureau) and Sue Chang of Dow Jones MarketWatch (San Francisco Bureau) for agreeing to review my book and give me their invaluable reactions and feedback prior to publication.

I would like to thank Alap Shah and James White at Sentieo for graciously providing access to stock market data, Tom Kang, Neil Shah and Peter Richardson at Counterpoint Technology Research for providing access to mobile device industry data used in this book, and Atlas Kuo of inSpectrum for his friendship and help with the memory semiconductor industry. Industry experts Sandesh Patnam and Elaine Kwei were kind enough to look through my book to offer their impressions. Marco Chen and Billy Kim, both of whom previously worked with me, were kind enough to give me their honest reactions and advice. Last but not least, I must thank Mark Edelstone for recruiting me into the world of equity research in the first place.

With sincere thanks and best wishes,

Sundeep Bajikar

What this book is not (please do not buy this book for the wrong reasons):

While this book contains discussions of technology industry trends across semiconductor, hardware and software/internet, it is not intended to serve as a comprehensive handbook or primer for investing in technology stocks. The book is certainly not intended to communicate any sort of "get rich quickly" schemes. Also, while this book is written with individual investors in mind, the processes discussed in this book are not intended to be of a "do it yourself" nature (e.g. this is not "Equity Research for Dummies", or "DIY Equity Research"), and should not be interpreted or followed as such. I strongly believe that individual investors whose primary occupation is not investing, should not own stocks based on their own independent research, except under supervision by a trusted investment professional. In fact one of the central recommendations of this book is for you to consider finding a trusted investment advisor to help you achieve your individual investment goals on a personalized basis. In that regard this book is notably different from other popular self-help investing books, including several books written by financial celebrities like Peter Lynch, recommending specific processes or algorithms to help individual investors select stocks for their portfolio.

Past performance is not a guarantee of future results.

Table of Contents

Preface

I decided to write this book for two reasons – 1) to inform and educate the individual investor and the public at large, and share my perspectives about the otherwise "black box" world of institutional equity research, and its clients, institutional investment managers; and suggest an approach for the individual investor to take advantage of deficiencies in the institutional system, and 2) to share a process that I practiced with considerable success, for analyzing investments in technology companies, during my 9+ year career as an equity research analyst, following a 9-year career in the technology industry, as an engineer. I believe the core elements of my process would be highly applicable to investments in other (non-tech) sectors as well. I have written this book with a broad audience in mind, from individual investors to career changers, to buyside analysts who might have been tasked with researching technology companies in particular. My hope is that the information and discussion in this book will also be insightful and perhaps entertaining to others that may not necessarily have a specific agenda but are nevertheless curious about the financial services industry.

I have noticed frequent misunderstanding and misperception of the role of a sellside equity research analyst (aka "stock analyst", "Wall Street analyst") working for an investment bank, perhaps because sufficient efforts haven't been collectively made to inform the public about the functions and responsibilities of the role, or frankly because a sellside equity research analyst isn't really supposed to have individual investors as his or her clients. It's a profession that isn't as well advertised to MBA graduates from top programs, as compared to transactional investment banking roles for example. It's certainly not a profession that I aspired to pursue growing up, and I am quite sure neither do others. For various such reasons, I don't think the average investor is well equipped to interpret research reports written by sellside analysts. Instead it would seem a lot more convenient to just blame the analysts for one's independent investing missteps.

When it comes to the buyside – and this I know first-hand as well, thanks to countless discussions with a range of highly intelligent investors around the world, relentless pursuit of short-term relative performance continues to reign supreme, perhaps based on an implicit assumption that such short-term relative performance is also of critical importance to individual investors. For example - if you lost 50% of your assets, would it matter if the stock market was down 60% and you outperformed the market? An individual investor is unlikely to find such outperformance impressive when faced with substantial loss of principal, yet a fund manager would tout such outperformance as basis for growing assets under management. Focus on the short term not only drives higher trading costs and management fees, but also a structural handicap; and resulting (often predictable) behavior by institutional money-managers creates opportunities for individual investors (or their independent wealth managers) to protect and grow their investments.

A better understanding of the cast and characters of the investment world should in theory enable individual investors to make more informed decisions about managing their investments. Specifically, my hope is that individual investors that read this book, would be encouraged to question their choice of stocks, mutual funds, or investment managers, in case they haven't executed a similar "house cleaning" recently. Having an investment manager whose interests and goals are aligned with your own, is obviously important to your financial success. It fascinates me that individuals work very hard through their lives to earn substantial amounts of cash, only to hand it over to money managers (e.g. mutual funds) that on average have different goals than those individuals whom the cash belongs to. The financial services industry I think thrives on the ignorance of its clients, especially individual investors.

I have been a student of the philosophy of value investing, which of course was established, executed, and popularized by superinvestors Benjamin Graham, Warren Buffet, and Seth Klarman among others. In this book I describe a research process that applies the tenets of value investing to the task of identifying profitable investments in the technology sector. The punchline here is that if you have a strong academic and/or industry background in technology, understand how disruptive new high-tech products are created, and other politics of the tech industry, then you stand to have an advantage over the average professional investor in evaluating investments in tech stocks, assuming you can also gain mastery of the research process, and remember to follow process discipline at all times. That may of course be a lot to ask for, especially if identifying investments or managing money is not your primary occupation – it isn't for most people. Still, insight into such a process that a skilled investment manager could execute on your behalf, should provide more visibility (and therefore comfort) into a mechanism that would be used to protect and grow your investments.

Here's what I hope to gain from writing this book – 1) satisfaction that I have made an effort to help my family, friends, and well-wishers understand what I did for 9+ years of my career in equity research, and why I was too busy to spend more time with people that wanted and deserved my company, 2) a basis for mutually rewarding personal and professional relationships as a trusted advisor, and 3) a codified reference for process elements that I diligently developed and practiced but didn't previously have a chance to document. Deep in my heart I would like to help individual investors by sharing my knowledge and experience, even if for a small fee, because I strongly believe in two things – 1) individual investors whose funds are being managed deserve to know the process of investing and the basis for selecting specific investments being made on their behalf, and 2) sharing investment theses for individual stocks (and the process behind developing such theses) with individual investors would only reinforce process discipline by allowing the validity of such investment theses to be re-examined frequently. These are not standard processes followed by the average active investment manager today, and my hope is that this book serves as a change agent in that regard. Investment managers should be held to a higher standard, not just per force through compliance, but also through active education of individual investors.

I expect about a third of the readers of this book to dismiss it as common knowledge. I expect another third of the readers to find the information presented either incomplete, too abstract or difficult to follow. I expect the remainder of the readers to find the book interesting, if only for its chosen presentation format filled with illustrations, and I expect that a portion of these readers will seek out assistance from an investment manager to apply their learnings to their investment portfolios.

The process of identifying and managing investments should involve a lot of discussion, to make sure that the key assumptions or objectives are well communicated and mutually understood. In that spirit, I have included below advice for contacting me, should you have follow up questions or need help. Keep in mind that this book comes with FREE access to additional online resources such as case studies and stock pitch examples – see website information below.

Advice for contacting me:

Readers: sundeep@bajikartechinvestor.com

Case Studies, Stock Pitch Examples: www.bajikartechinvestor.com

LinkedIn: www.linkedin.com/in/sbajikar

Twitter: @SundeepBajikar, #bajikartechinvestor

Facebook: www.facebook.com/ertechinvestor

Tumblr: http://blog.bajikartechinvestor.com

Chapter 1 – INTRODUCTION

A Journey in Value Investing

It was late-2007. After spending about a year at Morgan Stanley in Semiconductor Equity Research, I had started to become a bit disillusioned about my job, and was questioning if my transition from the technology industry to finance was the right move. Actions of people around me were not making a lot of sense. To be clear, Morgan Stanley ("the firm") at the time was regarded as the top investment bank for Technology-related banking and research. I received a lot of training on "how to make stock calls", "how to identify and influence key investment debates", "how to estimate what was baked into the price of a stock", etc. after having cleared four licensing exams (Series 7, 63, 86, 87) – a requirement for equity research analysts employed by broker-dealers. In theory I was extremely well prepared for my job. But something was missing – there was no clear sense of purpose, and I struggled to relate to the newly received financial training, as an individual investor. Scurrying around to make sense of every incoming news headline, coming up with something intelligent to write about it and what it meant for stock prices of companies we had under coverage, and updating models with our "insightful" forecasts I thought was borderline insanity – an effort to create something out of thin air, unlike the products I was used to developing at Intel Corporation. To think that someone, if anyone, was deriving tangible value from my work was unimaginable. That's when I found comfort in going back to reading books on Value Investing, just before the financial crisis of 2008 hit.

I distinctly remember sitting at my desk and watching the red ink covered stock screen for days and weeks, as investors were fleeing from just about every stock or bond out there. Morgan Stanley itself was caught in the financial storm quite badly. We were all clinging to our chairs watching Morgan Stanley stock sink real-time to $8 from ~$40, as Bear Stearns and Lehman Brothers went out of business, while the media continued to scare investors, as if everyone wasn't already worried. The stock stabilized and started to recover only after Morgan Stanley was able to get a capital injection from Mitsubishi UFJ of Japan, and after the government announced its bailout of financial firms. In the spare time that I had from all the excitement, I was busy buying beaten down securities that I fortunately had already identified, thanks to my nearly one year of study of value investing – just in time for the financial crisis. Those securities by the way, appreciated by 50%-to-100%+ over the following two-to-three years – not a bad outcome at all, not to mention of course the market as a whole also recovered nicely. My only regret is not having deployed significantly more capital for the investments that I made – I was still in early stages of testing my value investing skills, and clearly lacked enough confidence to take full advantage of the situation. As of the writing of this book, the world is once again navigating a financial storm – the culprits might be a bit different this time, but for me, reactions I am seeing in the stock market and in the media, are reminiscent of the 2008 crisis. And it's a good time to apply value investing aggressively again – to technology stocks.

I left Morgan Stanley in early-2011 to expand my coverage and build my own research franchise at Jefferies, where I had the chance to cover a unique mix of Semiconductor, Semiconductor Capital Equipment, and IT Hardware stocks that together made up nearly a trillion dollars of market cap. As a smaller firm, the culture at Jefferies was a lot more entrepreneurial and flexible – just what I needed to apply my process for consistently finding value in technology stocks. I left the sellside in late-2015; and as of writing this book, I am managing my own portfolio of investments, as well as consulting with other independent investment managers.

The book starts out with a description of the cast and characters of the financial system. To make investments comfortably and confidently over a lifetime, I believe that having an understanding of who you are up against is invaluable. Unless you have worked for an investment bank for a few years sometime in the last ten years, I would encourage you to read Chapter 2 – the industry has changed, and is changing, and a number of market participants don't fully understand the lay of the land – an unnecessary handicap to have. I truly believe that the individual investor (or investment manager) can take advantage of the institutional financial system over and over again to maximize their returns.

In Chapter 3 you will find discussion on a key tenet of value investing – focus on absolute returns (not relative returns). But to accomplish this in a repeatable fashion while minimizing risk, requires a disciplined process. I share my process in Chapters 4 and 5. If you have any training in security analysis, you will find these chapters very familiar. However, my process involves subtle differences, which ultimately I think make a big difference in the investment outcome. Like Warren Buffet has famously said – successful investors know how to do simple things exceptionally well.

As you may infer from reading this book, I did not learn the value-biased process described in this book from anyone on the sellside, though of course everyone I interacted with had invaluable influences on me. Chapter 6 builds on this further with another key tenet of value investing – margin of safety. I have provided illustrations to help drive home the concept of margin of safety, as well as a process for assessing margin of safety in technology investments – this I think is different from other value investing books that perhaps have not focused as much on the exciting world of technology investments.

In Chapter 7 I discuss issues related to international stocks, using Samsung Electronics as a case study.

In Chapter 8, I share my view of several important technology industry dynamics, as examples of investment themes that could be used to narrow down stock selection. Again you will find multiple case studies to demonstrate how uncovering important industry dynamics can drive lucrative investments in growth stocks. Yes, confusing institutional nomenclature notwithstanding, value investing does not exclude growth stocks.

Chapters 9, 10 and 11 provide a window into behavioral pitfalls in investing. Basically the point of these chapters is that we are our own worst enemies when it comes to investing, and learning to control our behavior can prove to be very profitable. As investors we have to constantly be aware of our deficiencies (I know that is hard), follow a disciplined and patient value investing process, and maintain a longer-term perspective. It is equally important not to get sucked into exotic investment schemes that promise consistent above-market returns, if you can't easily understand exactly how it will be done.

In Chapter 12, I provide a framework to think of different types of information available to investors, along with the sources of such information.

In Chapter 13, I propose an investment management framework specifically with the technology investor in mind, with two objectives – maximize investment returns within a compliant framework, as well as transparency between an investment manager and her individual investor clients.

Appendices 1 through 4 are intended to give you a brief overview of select tools and data services that I have used and found to be beneficial for investing in tech stocks.

I have posted stock pitch examples on my website bajikartechinvestor.com and readers of this book will have FREE access to those materials. Think of a stock pitch as the culmination of all the hard work in equity research, with a specific recommendation to buy or sell a stock.

I have provided references to other books, primarily value investing books, to help you dig deeper into some of the concepts. I have hopefully provided just enough introduction and discussion of key concepts to be able to tell a complete story, but this book is by no means intended to be a comprehensive handbook of any sort. It also most certainly is not a "get rich quickly" scheme by any stretch, nor does it recommend specific securities to buy or sell.

Investment Time Horizon

Discussion in this book assumes an investment time horizon of 2-to-5 years or more, though in some cases the investment horizon may be less than 2 years due to the timeline of underlying business fundamentals. There are at least two main reasons for the longer-term time horizon –

1) The average investment horizon (aka holding period) for stocks is significantly less than 1 year. I discuss later in the book why that is the case – the principal reason is that market participants are increasingly behaving like traders rather than business owners or long-term investors,

and an important way to sidestep shortcomings of the average market participant is to invest with a longer holding period.

2) Business cycles can last roughly from 2-to-5 years (or more), and it could take that long for your investment thesis to play out and for value to be realized.

An additional reason to invest with a longer-term investment horizon is to maintain process discipline and resist getting seduced by temptations to trade in and out of stocks frequently. Fact is that no one knows which way the stock market is going to trade the next day, week, or month; so deluding yourself into thinking you know something about the overall market that others don't and trying to trade under that false assumption is I think a habit to be nipped in the bud. In fact in my experience, a great many market participants started out with the best of intentions, to be longer-term fundamentals-driven investors. However over time, they succumbed to either the temporary excitement of trading, or to short-term performance pressure, and admit to have turned into traders. If you think gambling is exciting or addictive, then you should think about stock trading in a similar vein, if it helps avoid falling into that trap. While it may be acceptable to some people to gamble with a relatively insignificant portion of their assets, perhaps for the thrill of it, the average individual investor would probably not want to see her assets serving as gambling fodder for her investment manager. The issue here is not necessarily that the investment manager might have bad intentions (usually not the case), but more likely that he might not be following process discipline, which involves among other things thorough equity research, and behavior control.

To Invest or Not to Invest

I have added this section on demand from a close friend, who thought it would be worthwhile for me to capture my views on this dilemma that many in the technology industry seem to have, given that they are seemingly earning a good income, and are happy saving their cash in the bank. Fear of the unknown is core to human psychology, and fear of investing is no different in that regard. To me, the question of whether or not to invest (e.g. in stocks) is not that different from other questions like – Should I work or not? Should I study or not? Should I maintain my health and fitness or not? Each is a form of investment of time, money, and other resources, with an expectation of a return much greater than the investment. I have often griped with friends that educational systems here in the U.S. and around the world simply do not do a good enough job teaching individuals how to (and why to) invest. One can easily graduate with a Master's degree in engineering, medicine, or even finance, without really knowing a whole lot about investing, even though investing is arguably a core skill for navigating life successfully – unless of course you are independently wealthy and have the luxury and vanity to just blow through your assets over your lifetime.

Investing is necessary to protect and grow wealth. Investing could be done with a specific targeted need in mind, such as retirement, a large purchase, college tuition, charity; or investing could be done more broadly to maximize the future potential of assets. More assets enable more opportunities and provide optionality, which is valuable. Investing also addresses the more fundamental task of preserving the purchasing power of today's earnings. Earnings accumulated in cash stand to become less valuable over time due to a number of factors including – currency devaluation, inflation, rising taxes, etc.

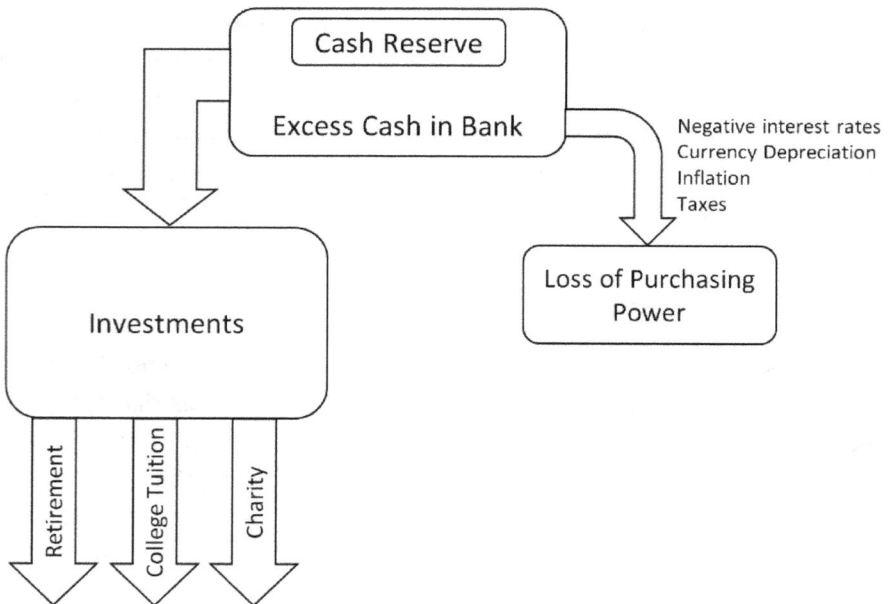

Through a detail description of the research process, I will try to make it clear why 1) investing without the support of proper research is akin to gambling, 2) proper research takes a lot of time and effort, as well as domain expertise in the case of technology, and other sectors like pharmaceuticals, 3) the average mutual fund or hedge fund will find it difficult to beat the market, and this means your returns from investing in these funds will be below the market's after fees. At any given time, there are only a small number of investment managers that are beating the market, and even fewer with a predictable, patient, and repeatable process. Finding the exact winning managers at the exact time in the short run is difficult if not impossible; certainly not feasible for the average individual investor. Even if you don't want to beat the market, but rather just want market exposure through an index fund or ETF, you are probably not going to be happy navigating periods of severe declines in market prices, and could benefit from timely advice driven by research. Unless you want to dedicate a substantial chunk of your time to researching investments and managing your own portfolio, you are going to want to recruit a trusted investment advisor who you believe can both understand and execute to your longer term goals and priorities.

How Investment Managers Make Money

Very simplistically there are two broad categories of investment managers – Institutional and Retail. The term institutional is used to refer to investment managers that cater to institutions – such as pension funds, insurance funds, and endowment funds. They often leverage similar investment strategies to provide their services to individual investors, also referred to as retail investors. This is typically done in the form of mutual funds or hedge funds. There is another type of investment manager who only caters to retail investors, without offering an institutional product. These investment managers often manage individual accounts hosted at brokerage firms like Charles Schwab or Fidelity. Investment managers working in private wealth management (PWM) departments of large investment banks like Goldman Sachs or Morgan Stanley, would fall under this retail category.

```
                    ┌─────────────────────────┐
                    │   Investment Managers   │
                    └─────────────────────────┘
                       ╱                    ╲
          ┌──────────────────┐      ┌──────────────┐
          │  Institutional   │      │    Retail    │
          └──────────────────┘      └──────────────┘
                                            │
┌──────────────────┐              ┌──────────────────┐
│  Fund of Funds   │              │    Individual    │
└──────────────────┘              │    Investors     │
                                  └──────────────────┘
   ┌──────────────────┐
   │  Pension Funds   │
   └──────────────────┘

      ┌──────────────────┐
      │   Endowments     │
      └──────────────────┘

         ┌──────────────────┐
         │  Insurance Funds │
         └──────────────────┘

            ┌──────────────────┐
            │     Trusts       │
            └──────────────────┘
```

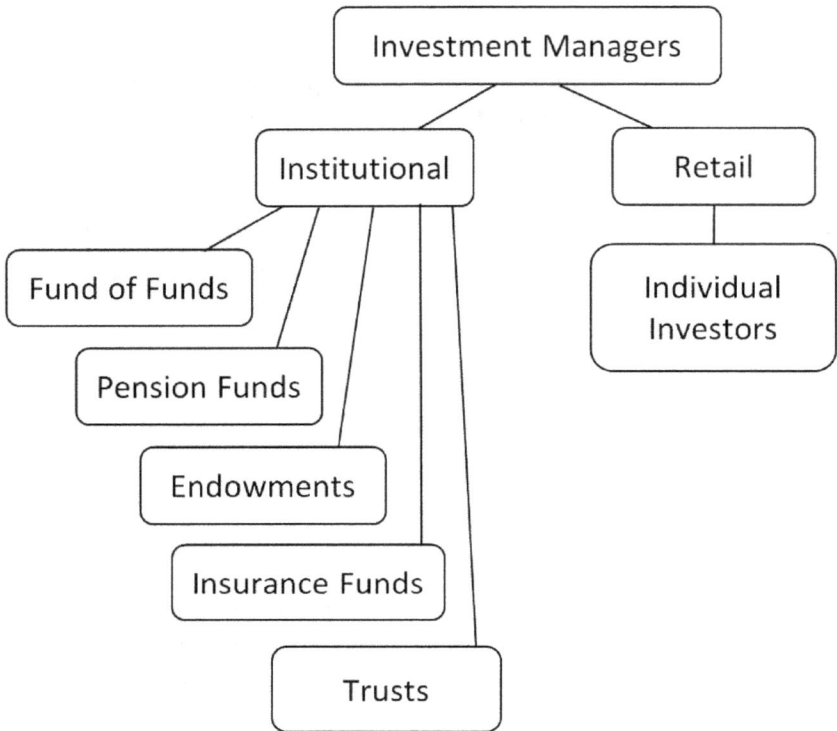

Investment managers can either be independent, or be affiliated with a broker-dealer such as Fidelity, Etrade, or Morgan Stanley. Independent investment managers generate income primarily by charging fees based on assets under management. Fees can range from 50 basis points (0.5%) to 300 basis points or more, depending on what type of suit the investment manager likes to wear! The more expensive the suits, the fancier the offices, the higher the fees – surprised? As assets under management (AUM) grow, so do fees, charged off a higher AUM base. In addition to such management fees, managers affiliated with broker-dealers also tend to be compensated on commissions charged for executing trades. In other words, it is not hard to imagine that a manager doing an excessive amount of trading in your account, stands to earn more in commissions compared to another manager who refrains from such "churning". Hedge Fund managers are notorious for additionally taking a 20% share of investment returns that they generate using your funds.

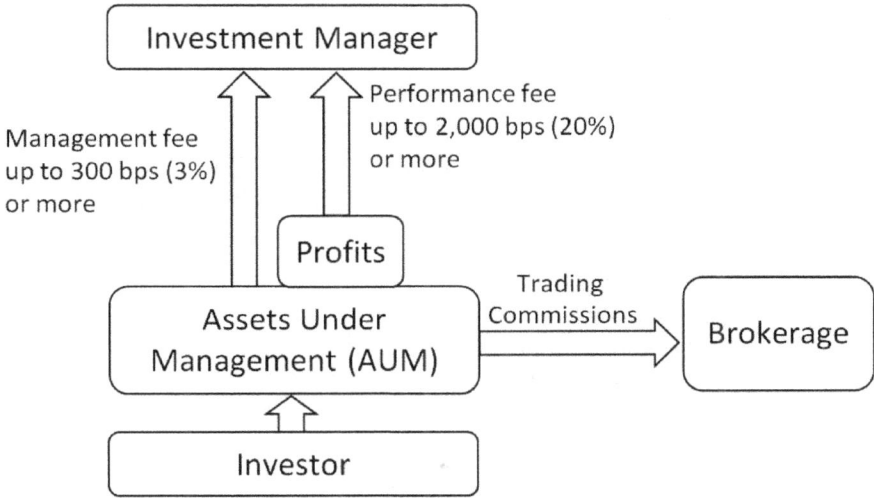

Guess what happens when your investments decline in value? Yes, managers still collect their fees. If there is one thing to take away from all this, it is that – you need to find a manager that you can trust to understand and execute an investment strategy that is consistent with your goals and priorities.

Finding an Investment Advisor

The most important elements involved in the selection process I think should include trust, depth of knowledge/experience, and investment style or track record. Word of mouth and testimonials are always useful, just keep in mind that what might work for your neighbor or friend or relative, might not work for you because you might have different goals or priorities for your investments. In general if you find someone with strong research credentials, with a longer-term investment horizon and a value bias, you are probably going to be on the right track.

Here are some questions to ask your prospective investment manager:

1) How do you select stocks for including in an investment portfolio?
2) Where do your stock ideas come from?
3) What is your process for analyzing investments (i.e. equity research)?
4) Who does equity research for you?
5) How much experience do you have in analyzing stocks?
6) What is your target holding period for each investment?
7) How do you determine whether you made an investment mistake, i.e. bought a stock that you shouldn't have?
8) What portion of the portfolio do you like to allocate to cash?
9) What is your definition of risk?
10) How do you manage risk?
11) What mistakes do you think most investors make often?
12) How do you avoid making those same mistakes?
13) Would you be willing to share your investment theses in individual stocks with me for my understanding?
14) Would you be willing to accept input from me about stocks to consider investing in?
15) Are you a sector specialist or generalist investor?
16) For sectors that you don't have special expertise in, how do you gain knowledge of industry dynamics?

Assuming a prospective investment manager answers all these questions, the next step is to determine what you are going to do with all the answers. While the answers are unlikely to be perfect by design, they should help you form a good idea of whether there is likely to be philosophical overlap between how you think and how the investment manager thinks. Having some overlap in thought process and investment philosophy would make the engagement more comfortable, but just how much overlap you need to be comfortable will vary across individuals. There is certainly value in having an advisor that thinks a little differently than you do.

Why Pay an Investment Advisor at all?

1) Because investing is not free – e.g. 100 trades in a year on a $300K account at $10 per trade cost ~30 basis points (aka bps - pronounced "bips"), more if you are purchasing mutual funds or

ETFs, which come with their own expense ratios of at least 20 bps, usually much higher. So paying ~100 basis points to an investment manager for all the personalized benefits you would get in return, doesn't necessarily seem like a lot. Anything higher than ~150 bps however does start to sound like you better know what exactly you are paying for.

2) If objectives are aligned, it can be a highly rewarding relationship, and you will have a trusted advisor to help you think through a range of investment decisions.

3) It is difficult to learn the necessary skills and behavior to become an equity analyst. If you are investing in individual stocks without first qualifying yourself as an equity analyst, then I'm afraid you might be gambling with your assets.

Asset Allocation

While the focus of this book is entirely on "bottom-up" technology stock selection, it is worth mentioning asset allocation as a "top-down" investment strategy that you may hear about. Asset allocation pertains to establishing an appropriate mix of different types of investments – stocks, bonds, ETFs, mutual funds, REITs, commodities, and cash, based on age, and other factors specific to an individual's risk tolerance. Retail brokerages and financial planners alike offer different levels of advice and assistance in determining your personal risk tolerance using a template of questions; and depending on the outcome, recommend various portfolio allocations. Many books have been written on the topic of asset allocation, which some experts have shown is responsible for >90% of portfolio performance, whereas only a small portion of the performance is driven by individual security selection. Depending on how asset allocation is implemented, it could represent an "active" or "passive" investment management strategy – more on that in Chapter 10, but I would agree in general that asset allocation is very important. The next chart illustrates the concept of asset allocation. As you can see in the chart, equity research which drives stock selection, is but one piece of the bigger investment puzzle, arguably the most important piece. Professionals who specialize in equity research are called equity research analysts (aka research analysts, stock analysts).

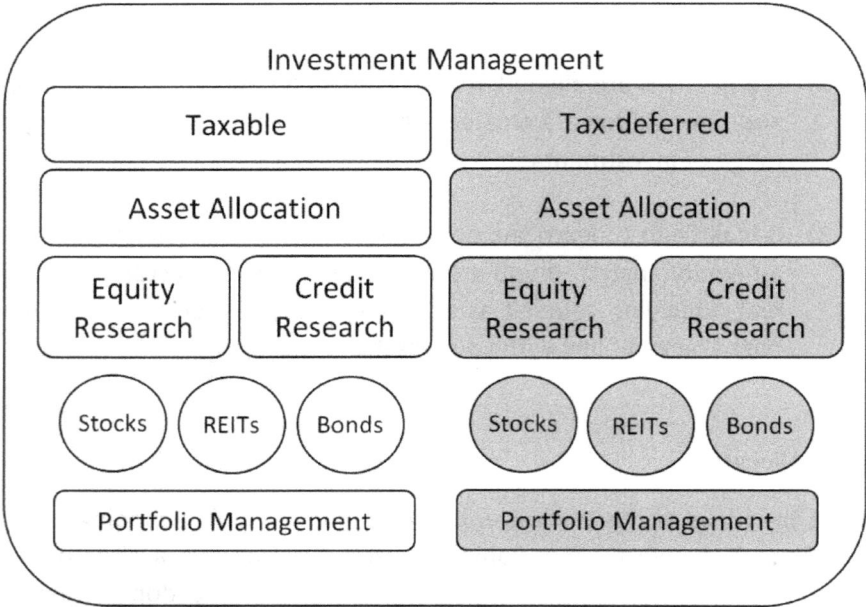

Investment Management

| Taxable | Tax-deferred |
| Asset Allocation | Asset Allocation |

Equity Research · Credit Research · Stocks · REITs · Bonds · Portfolio Management

Equity Research · Credit Research · Stocks · REITs · Bonds · Portfolio Management

How do you become an Equity Research Analyst?

The chart that follows captures the ingredients that I believe are needed to be a successful equity research analyst. Industry Knowledge and Behavior Control are the most difficult capabilities to possess, while Financial Analysis and Stock Analysis can be relatively easily learned.

Access to Data – this refers to a stock market data service, like Sentieo. Such a service provides access to financial data that can greatly expedite the process of building models, and analyzing what's baked into the stock price. Such activities along with processing company filings or press releases can be accomplished independently, but are greatly simplified and expedited through an integrated, Cloud-based data service like Sentieo. Traditional services like Bloomberg, Factset and CapitalIQ are expensive, and require you to learn their proprietary processes for accessing different types of data. I think with proliferation of Cloud services and Fintech business models, we are likely to see rapid disruption of the traditional model with new services like Sentieo.

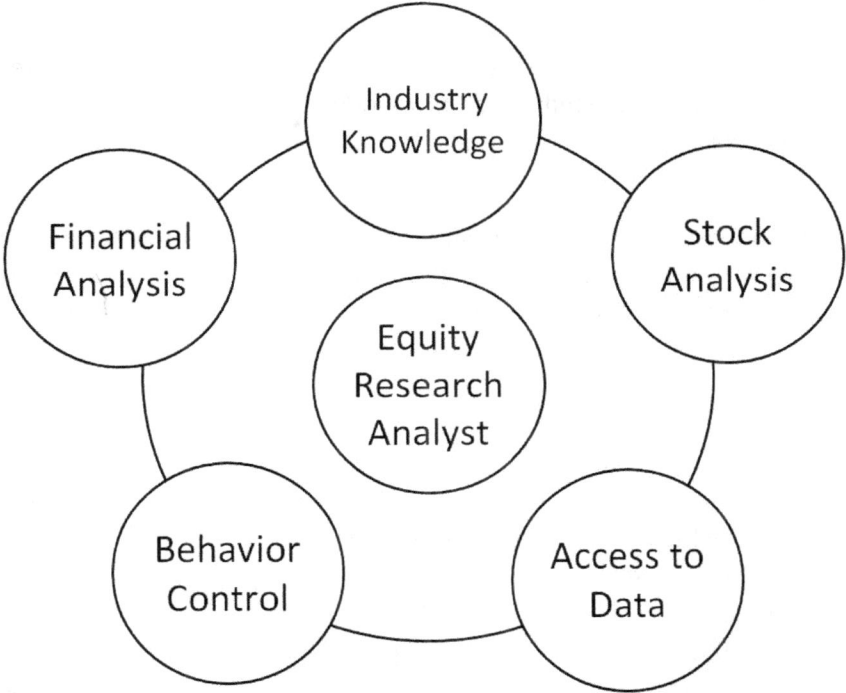

Finding a job in Equity Research either on the Sellside or on the Buyside is a topic that deserves its own separate book – perhaps I will get around to writing one. In the meantime I would be happy to consult with anyone who needs help. There seem to be a few books published on the topic; but since I haven't read any of them, I am not in a position to recommend any specific book.

Generalist vs. Specialist

A central theme of this book is that being a Tech Specialist who is able to combine deep industry knowledge with disciplined financial analysis, should generate a significant advantage over a generalist investor in Tech.

Case studies in this book will try to demonstrate this with data, but this idea became ingrained in me over many years, after observing countless such case studies in which I was consistently surprised by the lack of preparation of the generalist investor, as well as tech specialists who unfortunately weren't much better than generalists. I have met a number of impressively intelligent analysts in their own rights, but my point is that it is simply not possible to fake expertise in tech unless you have a tech background by way of studying and/or working in the industry – there are no short cuts.

On the bright side, if you have a tech background, it is relatively straightforward to acquire financial analysis skills, for example by pursuing an MBA with a Finance major, or the CFA program. After you earn your finance qualification you would need to find a position as a financial analyst, or a mentor who can show you how to put it all together.

My View on Stock Tips

In my view, recommending individual stocks on an off-hand basis to friends or acquaintances casually is like recommending prescription medicines without being a medical doctor – it wreaks of lack of responsibility. I believe the best way for me to help my friends, acquaintances, or clients, is to help them find a trusted investment manager. The process of discussing financial goals, approach and philosophy toward investments, as well as other constraints involved, should precede any individual stock recommendations. Ultimately the investment manager should be responsible for selecting individual stocks for you, consistent with your goals. You can always either question the investment manager's stock selection, or feed your individual stock ideas into your investment manager for screening. Actively contributing your knowledge and experience into the process of managing your investments should surely be a constructive and welcome element of the process. Imagine a world where every investor in a fund is actively contributing her insights so that her investment manager can incorporate them in the best fashion. Then think about how many mutual funds or hedge funds you know follow this approach. More on this in Chapter 13.

Below is a list of books that I have read, learnt from, and would recommend to readers of this book.

The Intelligent Investor, by Benjamin Graham, updated with new commentary by Jason Zweig, Fourth Edition - This is probably the best book I have ever read, in terms of the magnitude of impact it had on me as an investor.

Security Analysis, by Benjamin Graham and David Dodd – Value investing professionals regard this book as the "Bible" of value investing.

Margin of Safety, Seth Klarman – Seth Klarman is a very well respected and highly successful value investor, who runs a hedge fund called Baupost. The original book has been long out of print, but it may still be found in libraries. A brilliant book, very concisely and clearly gets across a number of very important points. I would recommend reading this book after first having read The Intelligent Investor and/or Security Analysis.

Your Money and Your Brain, Jason Zweig – As of this writing, Jason is a reporter and columnist for the Wall Street Journal, and one of my favorite authors. He writes a column called "The Intelligent Investor" in the journal.

Best Practices for Equity Research Analysts: Essentials for Buy-Side and Sell-Side Analysts, James Valentine – I had the pleasure of learning a number of the techniques taught in Jim's book first hand from him during my time at Morgan Stanley, where he was Director of Research. Sections focused on making stock calls are more relevant for sellside analysis, but the rest of the contents are more broadly applicable.

Unconventional Success: A Fundamental Approach to Personal Investment, David Swensen – This book describes problems with the institutional investment management system (e.g. mutual funds), and how individual investors can benefit from those institutional handicaps.

Warren Buffet and the Interpretation of Financial Statements: The Search for the Company with a Durable Competitive Advantage, Mary Buffet and David Clark – This book does a good job of specifically highlighting criteria that Warren Buffet has used to identify good investments.

The New Buffetology, Mary Buffet and David Clark – This book also describes criteria that Warren Buffet has used to identify good investments.

The Five Rules for Successful Stock Investing: Morningstar's Guide to Building Wealth and Winning in the Market, Pat Dorsey – All around good book aimed at individual investors.

The Big Money, Frederick Kobrick – This book provides a good description of buy and sell discipline.

Common Stocks and Uncommon Profits, Philip Fisher – The book provides a concise framework comprised of fifteen points of fundamental characteristics to look for in a company before selecting its stock as an investment.

Value Averaging, Michael Edelson – As the title suggests, this books describes value averaging, an alternative to dollar-cost averaging.

One Up On Wall Street: How to Use What You Already Know to Make Money in the Market, Peter Lynch – This book contains good advice on stock selection targeted toward individual investors. Peter's advice includes ignoring short-term swings in the market and focusing on the longer term instead.

The Big Short, Michael Lewis – This book provides a uniquely insightful and entertaining perspective on misaligned incentives in the financial services industry, with a focus on the credit (aka fixed income) side of things (i.e. it does not focus on the stock market). The book provides a critical view of the investment banking system in the U.S.

Fooling Some of the People All of the Time, A Long Short (and Now Complete) Story, David Einhorn – David Einhorn is a well-respected and highly successful value investor, who runs a hedge fund called Greenlight Capital. This book makes the case for why short-selling is a necessary dynamic in the stock market.

Data Sources

Data for charts presenting stock market information (stock prices, NTM EPS estimates) in this book were graciously provided by Sentieo. Sentieo is a new market data service, which I think is well positioned to disrupt and displace more expensive services like Bloomberg or Factset, by leveraging a superior Cloud-based framework for equity research. Appendix 2 provides a quick overview of Sentieo, which I think any independent investment manager would find interesting.

Appendix 3 introduces Counterpoint Technology Research, an industry research data provider specifically for the mobile device market. I have known the principals at Counterpoint for a few years, and have found their data to be comprehensive and well researched. Any investment manager looking for a solid foundation to build their analysis of the mobile device market on would find this section interesting. Data pertaining to iPhone and iPad product mix referenced in this book were graciously provided by Counterpoint.

Appendix 4 introduces inSpectrum, a technology industry consulting service based in Taiwan, with emphasis on semiconductors, specifically memory semiconductors. I have known the principals at inSpectrum for a few years, and have found them to be trustworthy. Data pertaining to the memory industry referenced in this book were graciously provided by inSpectrum.

It is probably worth noting here that while Sentieo, Counterpoint, and inSpectrum have generously provided data for this book, I have not received monetary compensation for highlighting their services in this book.

Objectives of this Book

It is my intent that after reading this book, you should gain:

1) A better understanding of the different types of players that you will encounter in the world of investing in public company stocks, and the inter-relationships among those players.

2) Knowledge of various types of conflicts of interest that arise among different types of investors and market participants.

3) A good understanding of the process that I practiced professionally for analyzing technology investments, based on application of tenets of value investing.

4) An overview of behavioral issues that complicate the process of investing in stocks, and why process discipline is important.

5) Appreciation for the fact that selecting and analyzing stocks is very difficult and time consuming, and should be entrusted to an investment manager whose interests and goals are likely to be aligned with your own.

6) Appreciation for the idea that having a strong background and industry knowledge in the technology space can help drive a better investment outcome from technology stocks, through partnership with the right investment manager.

Chapter 2 – LAY OF THE LAND

What is an Investment Bank?

An investment bank provides access to capital markets for corporations, by aiding in the issuance and trading of securities. The most commonly recognized types of securities are stocks and bonds, though there are various complex or exotic securities like derivatives that are used for purposes of hedging or expanding circulation of underlying securities. Some investment banks also provide access to capital markets for individual investors, through private wealth management divisions. Major investment banks like Goldman Sachs, Morgan Stanley, and Jefferies, are broker-dealers, and have securities trading businesses. Other types of broker-dealers like Etrade, Fidelity or Charles Schwab trade securities, but are not investment banks. The chart below illustrates the functions of an investment bank in a simplified format. Many of the major investment banks also provide retail banking services, which include checking and savings accounts, term deposits, as well as loans and mortgages.

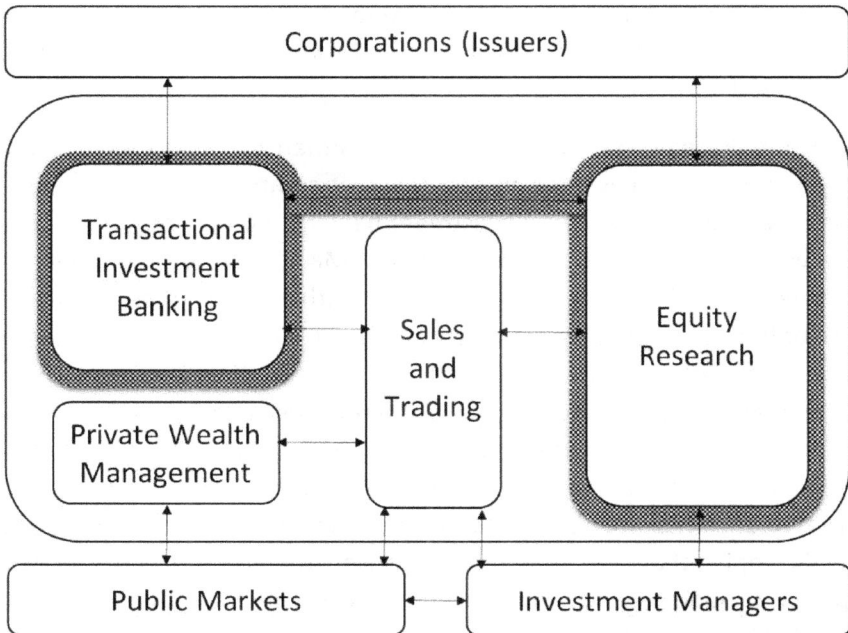

Referring to the previous chart, corporations like Apple and Google issue stock or bonds, and are also referred to as issuers for that reason.

The transactional investment banking division within an investment bank, is responsible for leading initial public offerings (IPO) of private companies, secondary stock issuances for public companies, as well as various straight debt or convertible bond issuances, collectively referred to as Corporate Finance. The transactional banking division is also responsible for advising issuers on mergers and acquisitions (M&A) deals. Advisory services provided by the transactional investment banking division for IPO, corporate finance, and M&A transactions generate fees or commissions, primarily from issuers. The red shading in the chart around the investment banking and research divisions indicates stringent information barriers put in place to control the flow of material non-public information in accordance with applicable securities laws. The investment banking division is routinely exposed to confidential information shared by its clients, which include private companies, as well as public companies. Such information is assumed to be shared by the companies under non-disclosure agreements (NDA), and is not meant to be shared with other divisions within the investment bank, such as equity research or sales and trading.

The Equity Research division within an investment bank is responsible for providing research coverage of two types of companies – (a) companies that have retained the firm's investment banking division for certain types of advisory services, with the exception of M&A, and (b) companies that are deemed to be strategically important either to investors, or to the firm, or both. Decisions regarding exactly which such companies should be covered are ultimately made by the firm's Director of Research. As shown in the chart, the Equity Research division routinely engages with all other divisions of the firm. Engagements between research and banking have to be chaperoned by someone from the firm's Compliance division, to make sure that such research-banking discussions within the firm are limited to specific topics that have been pre-approved for discussion. Such topics typically include vetting IPOs, or other corporate finance transactions being led by the banking division.

Sales & Trading

Sales and trading represents the lifeblood of the firm's securities trading business. Equity Sales teams interface with buyside firms (mutual funds, hedge funds, pension funds) to provide access to the firm's services, which include equity research, prime brokerage, corporate access, IPOs, etc. Trading generates commissions, which represent a major source of revenues for an investment bank. Trading is also responsible for market-making functions for certain securities, such as IPOs for example. Market-making means that the firm stands ready to buy or sell certain stocks with the intention of providing trading liquidity to the stock market.

Corporate Access is responsible for organizing events such as roadshows, and conferences, for equity research analysts as well as companies to engage with investors. Sellside analyst interactions with Buyside investors are referred to as "analyst marketing". Company (issuer) engagements with investors are called "company marketing" or "roadshow".

How does an Investment Bank Make Money?

The chart below illustrates the three primary mechanisms that an investment bank uses to make money. As simple as the chart looks, I can assure you that trying to understand exactly what combination of these and other methods a bank uses to make money, and exactly what conflicts of interest it faces, can be a very daunting task.

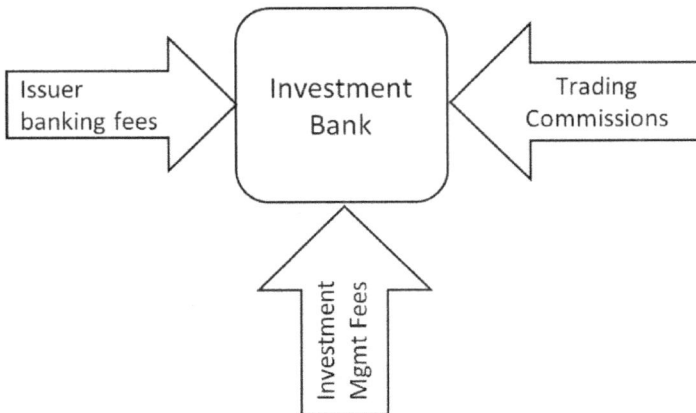

Issuer banking fees → Investment Bank ← Trading Commissions

↑ Investment Mgmt Fees

The Many Hats of a Sellside Equity Research Analyst

The next chart illustrates the multitude of functions that a sellside equity research analyst is responsible for, one of which is to analyze companies and write research reports. Functions shaded in green in the chart are not related to transactional investment banking, while those shaded in blue are related to banking. Almost everyone with the exception of individual investors and sellside analysts at other firms, can be looked upon as a potential client of a sellside analyst – this includes buyside investors, sales & trading, company management, as well as other industry participants. Having a variety of different clients affords sellside analysts the opportunity to have a broad range of conversations that serve to inform their views on specific companies as well as industries. Sellside analysts are typically responsible for covering a particular industry sector or sub-sector. Rarely is a sellside analyst given a chance to cover multiple sectors or sub-sectors. In a sector like Technology, a sellside analyst's client interactions are usually of a global nature, given the global reach of technology companies, as well as strong interest in U.S. technology companies from international companies and investors.

Almost everyone external to the investment banking system is often confused about the exact relationship between research and investment banking. Equity research analysts at investment banks are responsible for vetting certain types of transactions led and executed by the banking side of the firm. Initial Public Offerings (IPO) typically have to be approved/endorsed by the equity research analyst who would ultimately be responsible for extending research coverage to the concerned issuer upon execution of the IPO. In other words, if a research analyst determines through the vetting process that a company aspiring to launch an IPO would be unsuitable as an investment available to the public, or represents franchise risk to the firm underwriting the IPO, then the research analyst can recommend that the IPO be suspended or canceled. Research analysts are also involved in vetting certain corporate finance transactions like debt issuances. However, research analysts are not involved in vetting M&A transactions, and have no knowledge of such transactions until they are disclosed to the general public.

Analyst Marketing (Investor Marketing)

Sellside analysts routinely travel to meet their buyside counterparts around the world. This is called analyst marketing. The purpose of this effort is to deliver high-touch client service by bringing the most up-to-date research to the doors of buyside investors. The resulting conversations give sellside analysts a unique perspective of how market participants overall are thinking about a particular stock, and the sentiment surrounding a stock. Obviously no individual buyside investor can acquire such a perspective on her own, because she is not routinely meeting with a large number of her competitors. But she can certainly acquire a collection of such perspective from different sellside analysts servicing her. Depending on the topic or the stock, such discussions between sellside and buyside analysts can turn into highly charged debates – arguably such debates probably generate the most value for everyone by uncovering various perspectives and issues surrounding an investment.

Travel schedules for such analyst marketing tend to be highly demanding. Sellside analysts can be on the road for a total of up to three full months or more each year just for marketing. Each marketing day is typically filled with anywhere from four to eight or more meetings, and may additionally include group lunches or dinners to maximize time with investors. Often the analyst is also traveling to see investors, and that means there may also be a flight or two on a marketing day. It's probably not difficult for you to imagine that the highest concentration of investors occurs in locations like New York, Boston, Chicago, London, Hong Kong, and Singapore, and this is why more analyst marketing time is typically allocated to these regions relative to other parts of the world.

Non-Deal Roadshows

There are two types of roadshows – regular, and non-deal. Regular roadshows are hosted by transactional investment bankers with company management prior to company IPOs (i.e. while the company is still private). Non-deal roadshows (NDR) on the other hand are typically hosted by sellside analysts covering the companies. The purpose of a roadshow is to market the company to investors, by communicating its investment story succinctly and clearly.

The investment bank hosting the company's roadshow books meetings with the most relevant and appropriate investors that are most likely to be interested in investing in that company. Such targeting or match-making is led by the investment bank's corporate access department, with help from the firm's equity sales team covering the different investor accounts (i.e. mutual funds, hedge funds, pension funds, etc.).

Investor Conferences

Conferences provide a great opportunity for companies, investors, and sellside analysts to interact with each other at a higher level. Companies get a chance to tell their investment stories or provide topical updates – companies are typically given presentation slots, during which company presentations are hosted by sellside analysts covering them. During such presentations, company management is often interviewed by the sellside analyst covering the company, and Q&A from investors is encouraged. Following their public presentations, companies meet with investors in one-on-one or small group settings to further clarify their messages.

Conferences can last several days, and are typically hosted in comfortable locations that encourage plenty of informal interactions among attendees.

Such conferences can generate a wealth of new information, which sometimes has the effect of significantly moving stock prices.

Why Does the Buyside Need Equity Research Analysts?

The short answer is that the Buyside believes it can generate better tailored investment ideas through analysts directly on its payroll. Having your own analyst also means you don't have to worry as much about potential conflicts of interest that may impact research opinions provided by sellside analysts. Still, with the exception of a small number of buyside firms that completely shut out sellside analysts, buyside analysts tend to depend to varying degrees on input from sellside analysts.

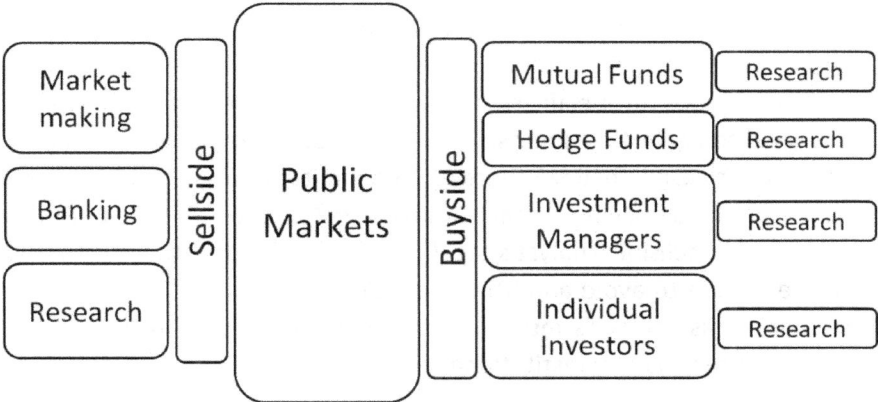

Sellside analysts typically cover ~10-to-20 stocks within a specific sector. Buyside analysts can be generalists, or sector specialists. A buyside sector specialist is typically expected to cover 30-to-50+ stocks within her assigned sector. Their higher relative focus on a smaller number of companies affords sellside analysts a better chance to develop more in-depth understanding of the companies they cover, compared to buyside analysts. I strongly believe that core equity research skills are highly transferrable from the sellside to the buyside, and vice versa. With that said however, I will also note a couple of practical problems that impede transitions from one side to the other. A number of buyside firms either implicitly or explicitly have a strong preference for hiring analysts that have previous buyside experience, and will exclude sellside analysts from

37

consideration. While I find this understandable when it comes to generalist positions, I don't fully understand why such a bias might make sense when recruiting for industry/sector specialist roles (e.g. Technology Specialist) – it may just be that people like to hire others that are like themselves. In the reverse direction, while the sellside might welcome buyside analysts to apply for open analyst positions, reality is that few buyside analysts have the pedigree or training or industry background to be credibly viewed as industry experts within the chosen sector on the sellside.

Compliance

In spite of adherence to heavily overbearing compliance processes that sellside analysts are forced to follow, some people still think that sellside analysts are faced with conflicts of interest when making recommendations on specific stocks. Except in the case of an IPO, where I would tend to agree that the risk of a conflict of interest might be higher, in most other cases I believe there is little institutional reason to assume there would be a specific conflict of interest. A more likely scenario that might affect a sellside analyst's stock recommendation I think would be his or her desire to avoid admitting a previously made mistake or error in judgment – this I think is much more an issue specific to an individual's behavior, rather than an institutional problem.

The mere possibility of a potential conflict of interest is so powerful however, that it has given rise to an army of compliance professionals, who are tasked with policing investment bankers and sellside analysts to make sure everyone is playing exactly by the book all the time. Regulatory oversight of such compliance processes is also getting more onerous over time.

Examples of compliance practices, which by the way are enforced in part through IT policies, include: locking down or limiting use of USB ports on company-provided desktop and laptop PCs to prevent unauthorized reproduction of sensitive content, elimination of expectation of employee privacy when using company devices, prohibition of access to personal email or online storage services when using company devices, severe restrictions on employee or family member stock ownership or trading, restrictions on participation in social media or talking to journalists, etc.

Equity Research Team Structure – Buyside

The chart below illustrates a general framework for how buyside investment teams are organized. One or more portfolio managers lead teams of senior analysts who may be tasked with analyzing specific sectors (e.g. Technology, Energy) or generally any security within the target market (e.g. U.S. large-cap equities, or emerging markets). Each analyst may report to one or more portfolio managers, depending on the needs in a given firm.

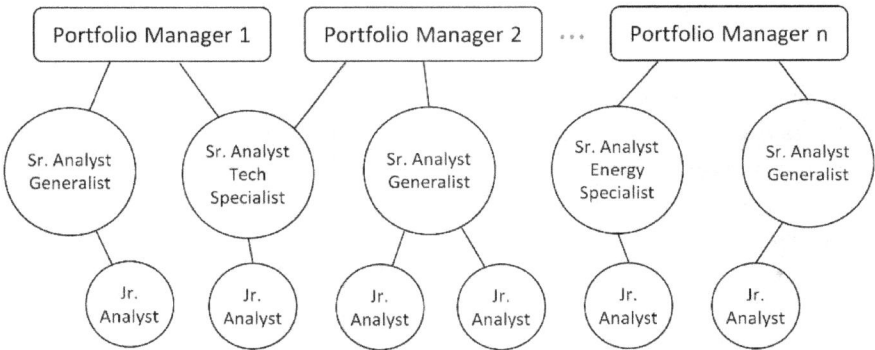

If you look into the hiring philosophy for institutional investment managers, you will find that on average they like to hire relatively inexperienced candidates (pre- or post-MBA) with at most 5 years of work experience, of which they like candidates to have spent 2 years in an investment bank, and a couple of years at another buyside firm. In other words, little to no importance is placed on sector-specific domain expertise or work experience when hiring for junior analyst positions. Larger firms occasionally hire senior analysts, who on average would have 5-to-10+ years of investing experience, but again there is a preference for prior buyside experience, even when hiring for sector-specialist roles. In other words, the buyside is structurally biased against its analysts having significant industry-specific knowledge in the form of industry work experience, and pursues a process of self-selection that leaves it with candidates that have more or less a similar profile across the buyside. No wonder then that the average buyside professional has limited understanding of the business operations of companies they invest in, and tend to gravitate toward businesses they have a better chance of understanding. Make no mistake — these are all extremely smart professionals, who are trained to invest using almost identical processes that are built on an implicit (or explicit) assumption that sector-specific expertise is worthless.

Equity Research Team Structure – Sellside

The organizational structure on the sellside is generally more consistent across the industry. Senior analysts (also called "lead analysts") are responsible for covering stocks within a pre-assigned sector (e.g. Semiconductor). Each senior analyst may have a team of one or more junior analysts (also called associates) supporting her in her coverage. Analysts report to the director of research, who is responsible for general people management, managing the interface with the firm's banking and other divisions, and determining which stocks or sectors the firm needs to cover. The next chart illustrates this organizational structure.

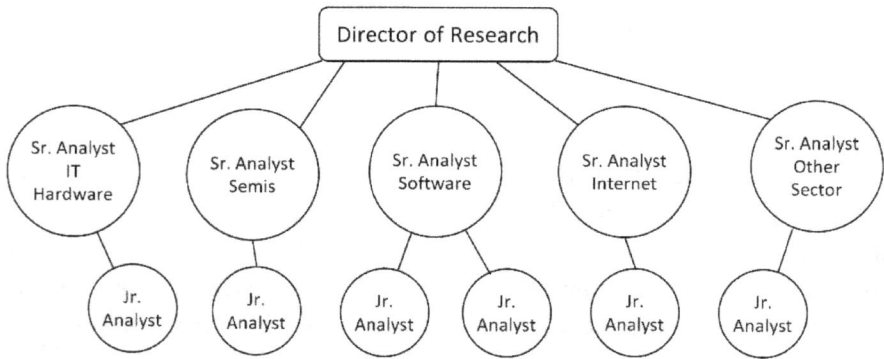

Turns out that the sellside has a little more recognition for industry-specific domain expertise, and you will often find sellside analysts that have previously spent a number of years working in the industries that they are covering. However, given there are dramatically fewer sellside firms compared to buyside firms, competition for such sellside positions is extremely high, and that makes it difficult for technology or other industry professionals to break into the sellside, except perhaps as junior analysts. Junior analysts may hold business titles like "Associate" or "Senior

Associate". Once a senior associate has proven that in addition to whatever domain-specific expertise she arrived with, that she can also analyze financial models, write coherently about company or industry dynamics, and effectively communicate such ideas to her clients, she is promoted to the Vice President level. Vice Presidents on the sellside may or may not have lead coverage of specific stocks. Beyond the VP level, analyst seniority is driven primarily by the market capitalization of companies under coverage, only because market cap is often thought to be suggestive of the level of impact or influence the analyst might have on her buyside clients. Other factors that may determine analyst seniority and/or compensation include – popularity among buyside clients (measured as number of votes received), reputation among company managements, etc.

The table on the next page provides a comparison between sellside and buyside analyst roles. As the table suggests, I do think that sellside analysts have a structural advantage when it comes to carrying out fundamental deep-dive research on individual stocks in a given sector, compared to their buyside counterparts, primarily owing to the elements highlighted in green shading in the table – focus and access. However, this does not necessarily mean that all sellside analysts should be looked at as experts in their sectors – due to a number of changes in the industry, allure of the sellside analyst position has faded. Also, given higher barriers to entry to become a sellside analyst, some incumbents have chosen to be on "cruise control", safely assuming that they cannot be easily replaced.

	Sellside Analyst	Buyside Analyst
Coverage	Sector focused, typically up to ~20 stocks	Generalist or sector-specialist, ~20-to-50+ stocks
Research approach	Primarily company and industry fundamentals	Varies: top-down macro driven, or fundamental
Publishing responsibilities	Publish research reports	No external publishing responsibilities
Avg. Time spent on each covered company	Higher	Lower
Access to Companies Under Coverage	Very good	Varies - large firms have good access
Reporting Structure	Director of Research	Portfolio Manager(s) and/or Director of Research
Analyst performance tracking	Publicly available	Not publicly available
Number of industry professionals	Fewer	Numerous
Barriers to entry	Higher	Lower
Compliance requirements	Higher	Lower
Analyst Compensation	Higher	Lower

Analyst compensation is not an easy topic to discuss except to say that there is no set formula to determine how an analyst gets compensated – this is especially true on the sellside, even though it is actually easier to measure sellside analyst performance on the basis of his or her stock recommendations, which are considered public information. Typically, performance of specific stock recommendations ends up being but one variable out of several, to determine how much an analyst should be paid. Other important factors, sometimes more important than stock performance, include – popularity among buyside investors (this is determined by counting votes), leadership and mentoring skills, trading commissions, and general helpfulness in supporting the firm's banking relationships. The last factor is worth clarifying, because according to securities laws, a sellside analyst cannot be directly or specifically compensated for any particular banking transactions. However, it is hard not to imagine that good sellside analysts attract company clients (issuers) to a firm. Research management is then faced with the fun task of figuring out exactly how to account for the value of the sellside analyst when it comes to support of the firm's banking business. As we discussed under the compliance section earlier, a firm's investment banking division is not supposed to have any influence on research analyst compensation (or hiring or firing or selection of stocks under coverage as well for that matter).

Ready to take on the investing challenge?

Armed with a more informed view of the structure of financial markets, you are better prepared to take on the investing challenge. In this jungle of sellside analysts, buyside analysts, equity sales professionals, company management, portfolio managers, and numerous other agents, it is impossible to precisely identify or measure the size of various dislocations or conflicts of interest that exist in the market at any given moment. This is why it is safer to conservatively assume that financial markets really can't be considered to be efficient over the short run, but perhaps have a chance to be efficient over a longer investment horizon.

In the next chapter I introduce the concept of value investing and lay the foundations for fundamental analysis, which drives absolute returns, and is the primary focus of equity research. The goal of equity research is to profit from identifying and capitalizing on short-term market inefficiencies that have high likelihood of correcting over the longer term. Investment returns are realized as market errors get corrected in the long run.

Chapter 3 – FUNDAMENTAL ANALYSIS AND ABSOLUTE RETURNS

Price vs. Value

Price is what you pay, for the value that you get in exchange. One premise of this book, as with the philosophy of value investing, is that the stock market is NOT efficient in the short term, but is usually efficient over the long term. This means that in the short term, market prices may not reflect underlying values of the assets that the stocks represent. This is precisely what creates opportunities for value investors to profit from arbitrage, selling stocks that are over-valued, and buying stocks that are under-valued. It also underscores the central theme of this book – equity research with the benefit of industry expertise in technology, should be able to uncover mispriced technology stocks better than both the ability of the market to efficiently price in every little fundamental detail, and the ability of the average investor to consistently uncover such mispricing.

Value Investing Defined

Value investing is the strategy of investing in securities (stocks, bonds) trading at an appreciable discount from underlying value. That is a simple sounding but loaded statement. As the founders of value investing have said, the greatest challenge in value investing is maintaining the requisite patience and discipline to buy only when prices are attractive and to sell when they are not, side-stepping the short-term performance frenzy that market participants seem to be perpetually consumed by. Embedded in value investing are at least three major tenets – the most important tenet is the idea of buying with a margin of safety; and the process of assessing margin of safety in technology stocks is covered in detail in Chapter 6. Focusing on margin of safety and minimization of risk of permanent loss of capital by definition leads to an investment strategy that maximizes absolute returns while minimizing risk, paying little if any attention to comparisons with some arbitrarily defined index of stocks.

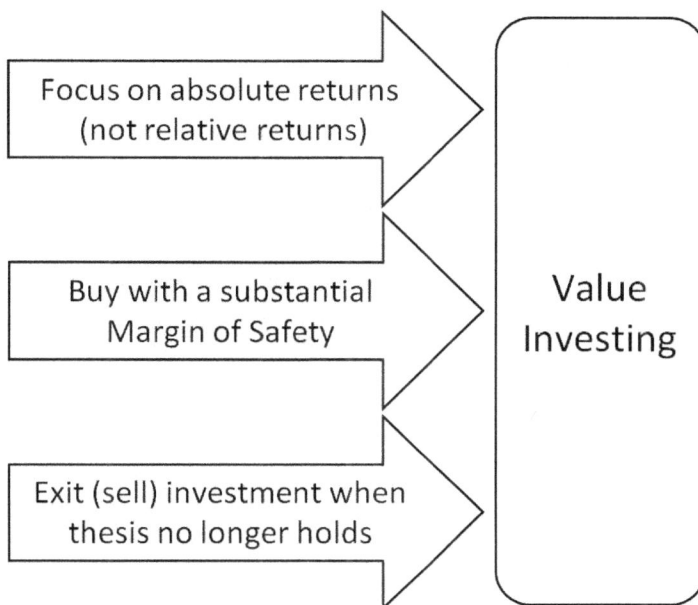

Focus on absolute returns (not relative returns) → **Value Investing**

Buy with a substantial Margin of Safety → **Value Investing**

Exit (sell) investment when thesis no longer holds → **Value Investing**

A key part of realizing gains through value investing is to exit an investment promptly after its underlying investment thesis has played out, and original margin of safety assumptions are no longer true because stock prices have moved significantly. Value investing disagrees with the Capital Asset Pricing Model (CAPM) or Modern Portfolio Theory (MPT), both of which are well taught in business schools, well regarded in the industry, and widely adopted as elegant mathematical frameworks that collectively suggest that higher investment returns cannot be had without undertaking greater risk.

Risk vs. Volatility

CAPM and MPT are based on a fundamental assumption or hypothesis that capital markets are efficient at all times, i.e. everything there is to know and understand about the world and about any individual company is instantaneously and continuously incorporated in the current market price of a stock. In other words, CAPM and MPT postulate that the market price of any stock at any moment in time is a true and accurate reflection of the underlying value of assets represented by the stock. Consequently, market participants, especially those with freshly minted MBAs, or those who have not had a chance to consider value investing, routinely use the terms "risk" and "volatility" interchangeably. Volatility is defined as the variance (standard deviation squared), a statistical measure of movement, of the price of a stock. Risk on the other hand is the probability of permanent loss of capital. Clearly, while the price of a volatile stock can fluctuate a lot in the short term, it says very little if anything about the probability of permanent loss of capital over a longer term investment horizon.

What drives stock prices?

The graphic below illustrates the different forces that are in play to determine stock prices at any given time. Since market participants generally agree it is impossible for any individual or even machine to precisely calculate the effect of such forces at any given time, short-term stock prices are widely understood to exhibit random behavior. The "short-term" by the way could be a period that spans up to a year or longer.

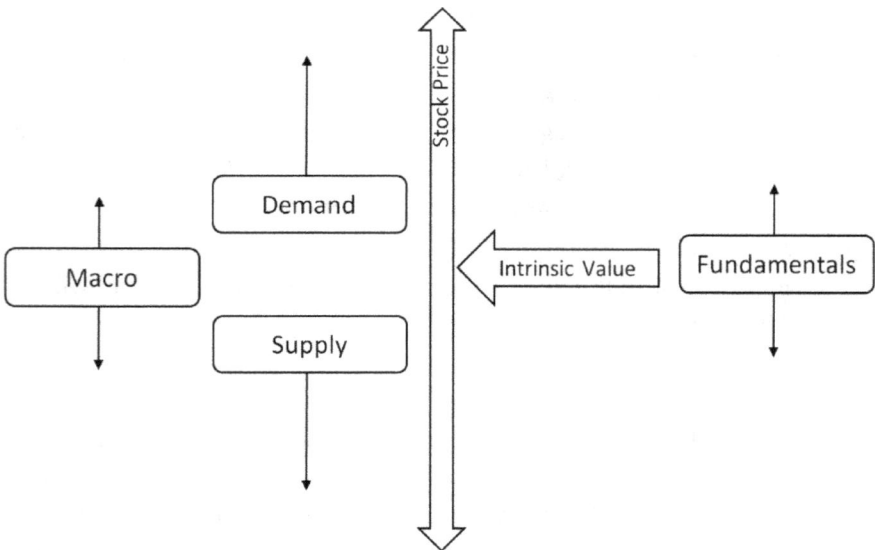

Even if you assume that every market participant has a full and complete understanding of fundamentals for a given company (this is usually never the case), they are unlikely to agree precisely on what the valuation should be. Once you step beyond the individual company and its stock to the broader market, you will find vastly differing views among market participants about a range of subjects that together make up the "Macro" outlook. This includes views on domestic and international interest rates, GDP growth, geopolitical factors like elections, wars or other complications, oil prices, other commodity prices, real estate, and a number of other topics. Even if all market participants were miraculously aligned on their macro views, it would still be impossible to predict which market participants would have a need to buy or sell the stock in question for reasons other than fundamentals, i.e. asset allocation, liquidity, or one-off events that trigger unpredictable stock market activity.

Equity Research Focuses on the Individual Company and its Stock

The purpose of equity research is to identify individual securities through fundamental analysis of underlying businesses. By definition then the focus of equity research is on the company, its business, and industry dynamics surrounding its business. While linkages to the broader macroeconomic picture may be established, the focus of equity research is not on forecasting macro, or GDP or other related parameters.

Stocks are typically owned as part of an investment portfolio. A portfolio may be designed to outperform a chosen index (e.g. S&P 500), or to generate absolute growth of invested assets. Given the short-term focus of institutional investors at large, with average holding periods of ~1 year or less (and trending lower), the sellside is accustomed to providing recommendations with an implied time horizon of ~1 year. However, in addition to fundamental problems with the sellside's approach toward research, recommendations issued by different investment banks are not necessarily directly comparable with each other. Banks follow different rating systems, with a mix of relative and absolute ratings, and this complicates the process of measuring analyst performance.

Examples of absolute ratings: Buy, Sell, Hold.

Examples of relative ratings: Overweight, Underweight, Underperform, Equalweight.

Some investment banks have decided that they can add even more value by interpolating the scale and adding a couple more ratings. Here is one example of such an extended rating system: Strong Buy, Buy, Market Perform, Sell.

A Sellside Perspective – Why Hold or Neutral or Equalweight Ratings are necessary

People expect equity analysts to come up with "actionable" recommendations, which they believe means "Buy" or "Sell". Indeed this is also what equity analysts strive for; but realistically it is not always possible to intellectually honestly assign anything other than the equivalent of a Hold rating to a stock. As frustrating as a Hold rating is to everyone, not the least of which to the analyst providing that recommendation, it serves an important purpose – to advise people not to Buy or Sell the stock at present levels, but rather wait for a better situation to develop over time.

Next let's consider a couple of examples of Hold ratings, and one example of a Sell rating. These case studies will help you start to form some idea of what fundamental analysis really means. Equipped with that knowledge, you will be in a better position to compare absolute return strategies with relative return strategies later in the chapter.

Hold-rating Case Study # 1 – Apple (NASDAQ: AAPL)

I was Hold-rated on AAPL from Sep-14 to Oct-15, while I was the senior analyst covering the stock at Jefferies. The primary reason for my Hold rating on AAPL was that investor expectations were elevated, and so was the risk of disappointment, and stock price decline. Even though I knew, like just about everyone else, that Apple was about to benefit from a strong product cycle with iPhone 6/6+, my assessment suggested the new product cycle would not necessarily be sufficient to keep up with the treadmill of higher expectations.

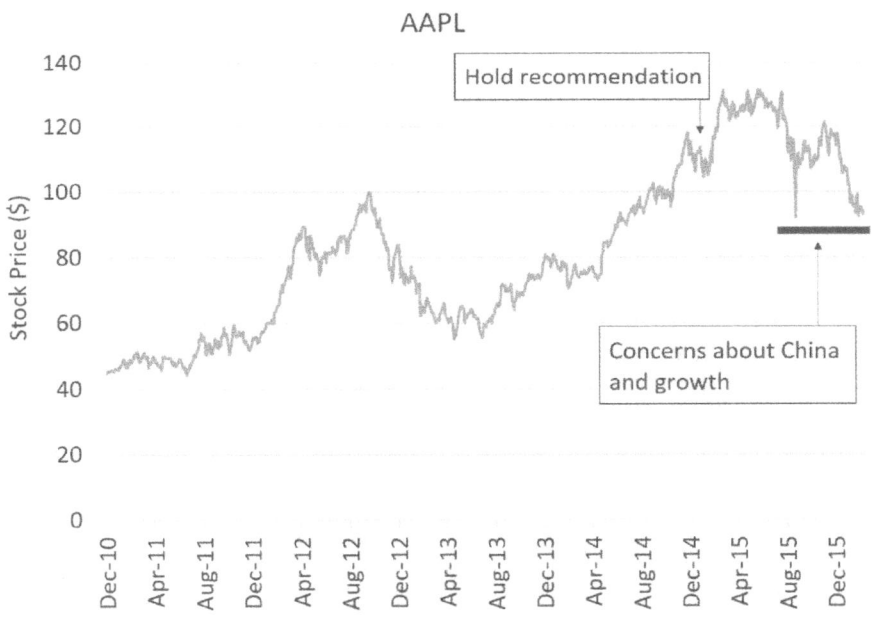

AAPL

From Sep-14 to June-15, Apple demonstrated dramatically better success selling its new iPhone 6/6+, particularly in China – results were so unbelievably good, that they handily beat the most bullish investor expectations out there. So the stock climbed, from $100 to $135. At that point Apple hit a speed bump. Investors began to realize that the massive growth spurt they had just witnessed was unlikely to continue; and from there it quickly turned into a problem of forecasting exactly when Apple would deliver its disappointment. Over the next six months, AAPL stock

49

gave up all those gains, and retreated into the low-$90s. As of this writing, the stock is treading water around mid-$90s. So looking back, the alternative to my Hold rating would have been a Buy rating starting out in Sep-14, followed by a timely downgrade around June-15 – not only would the quick change in ratings (changes within 12 months) not have been consistent with my style and investment philosophy, but it would also have required extremely precise market timing skills, which of course I was quite confident I never possessed.

Hold-rating Case Study # 2 – EZChip (NASDAQ: EZCH)

I think I committed Hold-rating sacrilege by being Hold-rated on EZCH, from mid-2011 until EZCH was acquired by MLNX in 2015. Over that period EZCH's stock price declined more than 50%. So clearly in hindsight I was wrong, and I should have been the equivalent of Sell-rated on the stock instead – with that admission of mistake, what I want to highlight here is the circumstances that led me to the Hold rating in the first place. In 2011 when I started covering EZCH, it was a relatively well-loved stock. What that means, is that investor expectations were already quite high. I remember walking into Hedge Fund meetings, and getting ripped up for not being Buy-rated on EZCH. At the time, EZCH was trading in the mid-$30s, and investors were hoping to ride it to >$100. See the chart below.

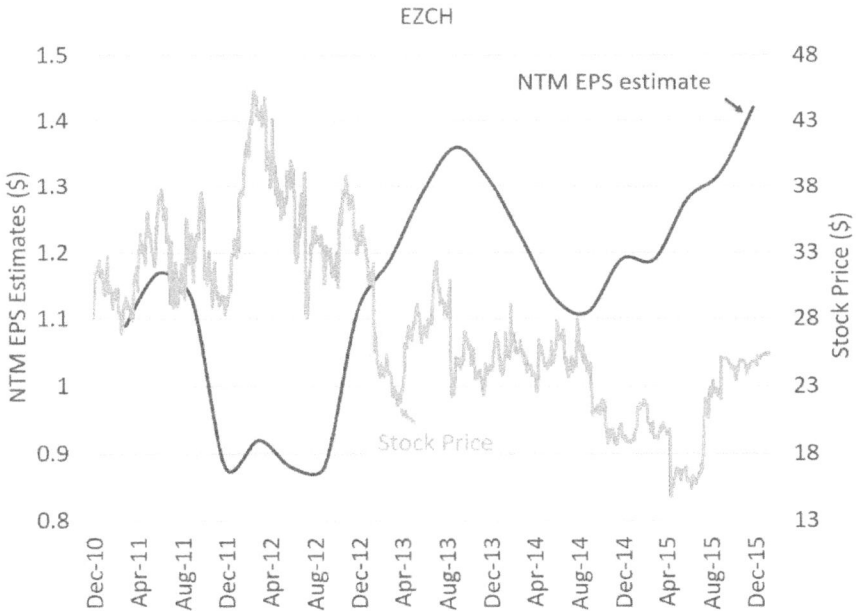

EZCH

As we saw with AAPL above, there was nothing fundamentally wrong with EZCH. The company had good products, it was executing well, and delivering good growth. However there was a problem with the company's marketing message to investors – it was perhaps too good to be true. Can you think of a company (in any sector) that can perpetually grow both shipments AND selling prices at double digits every year? Just because the company had enjoyed the benefit of strong revenue and pricing growth in its recent history was not a good enough reason to assume such dynamics would continue indefinitely into the future. Yet investors had bought the story exceptionally well. The funny thing here is that among the "smart money" hedge fund investors, there probably wasn't a single person that actually had a good understanding of EZChip's products. If they did, they would have realized that EZChip's biggest customer Cisco was unlikely to pay 2x prices with each upgrade for future generations of the same product it was using in its Edge Routers. EZCH stock climbed from mid-$30s in late-2011 to mid-$40s in early-2012, before it started losing steam, and fell all the way to mid-teens in 2015, just before it was acquired by MLNX for $25.

Sell Rating Case Study – QCOM's predictable structural problem

Even though I never explicitly issued a Sell rating on QCOM, because I did not have a chance to cover the stock as a lead analyst, my views on Qualcomm's chipset business fundamentals have been generally well known among investors following my work, and would have supported issuing a Sell rating on the stock, had I covered it at that time. See the chart below.

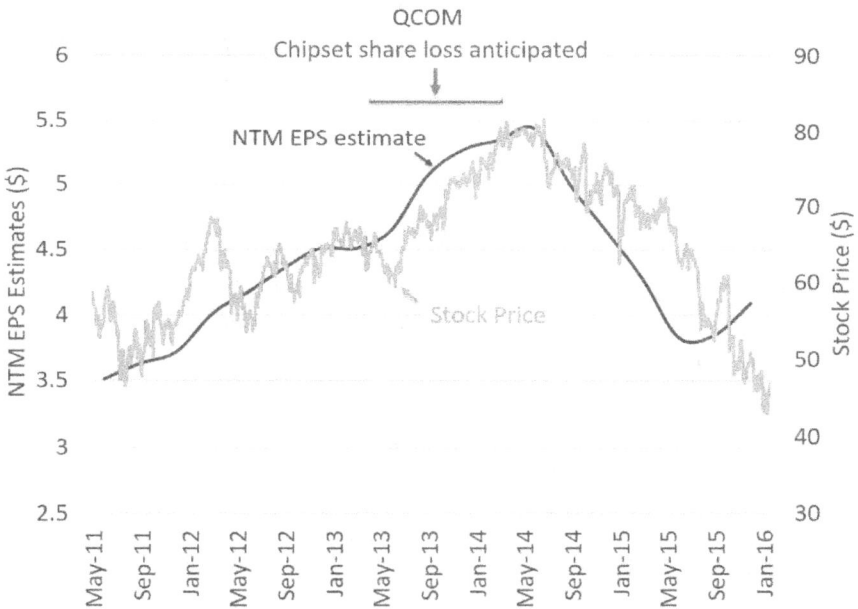

Due to my coverage of Samsung Electronics, I did a lot of work in the leading-edge foundry space – this refers to semiconductor contract manufacturing using the most advanced fabrication technology, commonly referred to as "leading-edge". The fundamental dynamic that I was analyzing was the likelihood of Samsung Electronics disrupting industry leader TSMC, by offering a more advanced technology solution at similar or lower prices.

Manufacturing semiconductors has long required the use of photo-lithography technology (a dramatically more advanced version of desktop photo printing). As you can imagine, the smallest feature size a lithography machine can "print" on a silicon wafer is a function of the wavelength of light used for the application. Over the last few years, advances in lithography haven't advanced the use of a finer wavelength of light to enable printing smaller chip features, and this is making it difficult for industry leader TSMC to stay on its historical path of "shrinking" chip sizes to deliver manufacturing cost reductions. When industry leaders can no longer maintain a technology advantage, it opens a window for competitors to catch up. This is exactly what Samsung Electronics achieved by delivering a more advanced 14nm FinFET manufacturing technology in late-2014, and disrupting Qualcomm in the process.

Qualcomm has been the "arms-dealer" supplying the brains in the form of Application Processor (AP) and/or modem chips powering the Smartphone revolution. It was also TSMC's largest customer. Starting in late-2012, TSMC's external technology presentations laid out its strategy, which went unnoticed by investors. TSMC was telling the world that after making a large investment at its 20nm node, it would not make another big investment to deliver cost reductions for its 16nm node. TSMC's investments at its 20nm node were also largely driven by its newly acquired customer Apple. As a result, Qualcomm was effectively shunted out of its critical leading-edge manufacturing relationship with TSMC.

Samsung was smart to seize the opportunity to accelerate its 14nm node development, as well as its internal AP alternative to Qualcomm's Snapdragon, both of which culminated in Samsung using its internally developed AP manufactured on its 14nm node for its Galaxy S6 Smartphone, which launched in early 2015. Additionally Samsung also introduced its internally developed modem alternative to Qualcomm's, across major markets with Galaxy S6. This represented a significant loss of business for Qualcomm, given Samsung was Qualcomm's largest customer. Worse, it solidified Samsung's entry as a merchant provider of AP to other Qualcomm customers, as a superior and potentially lower-cost alternative. What if Samsung is successful in supplying an AP using air-interface technology (modem) that doesn't generate royalties for Qualcomm?

I uncovered the potential for such chipset share loss for Qualcomm during my work on Samsung's foundry progress in 2013 and 2014, nearly two years before it actually played out. Qualcomm also separately faced challenges in determining whether it could collect royalties from customers in China – that portion of Qualcomm's problems was not core to my chipset share loss thesis, but also contributed to QCOM stock's subsequent decline. I spent much of 2013 and 2014 debating with investors around the world the challenges that Samsung's 14nm foundry success would pose for TSMC, Qualcomm, and others. Investors disagreed with me almost universally. It was very interesting for me to watch, knowing fully well that virtually all of those that disagreed with me really hadn't done much independent work or analysis on the topic. Worse, a large portion of those that disagreed were subscribed to canned marketing messages from the companies in question, and refused to dig even one level deeper.

Growth vs. Value Funds – The Unnecessary Dilemma

Value investing as referenced throughout this book, is the process of buying attractive investments at deep discounts. You will often find mutual funds classified as "growth" or "value", and this introduces confusion about their chosen investment philosophies at play. The process of value investing isn't defined to exclude high-growth companies, though high-growth companies tend to trade at higher valuations, at least when they are executing well, and this does make it difficult to buy them at deep discounts, until they deliver large disappointments. In other words, value investing can be applied to all types of companies, and having to make a choice between investing in a "value" or "growth" mutual fund shouldn't be necessary, if all the individual really wants is capital protection and growth. It's like asking if you want a fast car or a safe car.

Building Conviction

The process of building conviction in an investment idea is illustrated in the next chart. A critical part of building conviction is entertaining and welcoming opposite views. Chances are that if you started out bullish on a particular company, that you may not be able to independently come up with the most dire scenarios to assess downside risk for your investments. Reaching out to other investors, sellside analysts who are bearish on the stock, or reading the blogs, are ways to uncover opposite views. It is important to take opposite views seriously, form a good understanding of the fundamental scenarios they represent, and then assess the probabilities of those scenarios materializing over the investment horizon. This is easier said than done however, and bullish investors frequently dismiss bearish views, and choose not to prepare for adversity – this costs them dearly, especially in market downturns.

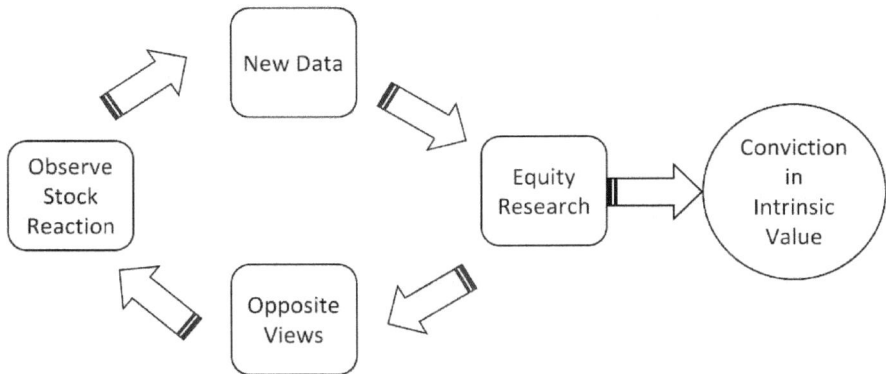

I have learnt that it is possible for various bear scenarios to depress stock prices over the short term, sometimes for legitimate cyclical reasons, or at other times for the fear factor they represent. In such cases, you have to make a choice – are you going to bail and run for the exits by selling your investment prematurely, or are you going to take advantage of short-term dynamics to raise your investment? The answer depends on how much conviction you managed to build when you had the chance and the time to do it.

Taking Advantage of Volatility

Market volatility is typically driven by broader macroeconomic concerns – whether it's an impending war, or economic slowdown, or busting of an asset pricing bubble. Market participants concerned about short-term returns (majority of market participants) do not like volatility, because in their investing frameworks, volatility = risk, which they try to sidestep by reducing their exposure to affected securities. When everyone sells at the same time, asset prices spike down, and often reach ridiculously low levels not justified by fundamental analysis along with a longer-term perspective.

Value investors who are prepared with thoroughly researched ideas, stand to benefit from such market volatility. Every time the market dips, value investors can run through their shopping list to see if any of the securities on it are at pre-determined levels of attractive prices. If so, either new positions can be established, or existing positions can be added to. If no bargains are available, the value investor can just wait for bargains to become available, while they continue their job of researching investment targets.

Institutional Obsession with Being Fully Invested

One byproduct of a relative returns strategy is the compulsive obsessive desire of investment managers to remain fully invested in stocks at all times. The persistent fear is that not being invested would cause the fund to underperform the market. Here again an absolute returns focus and a value philosophy is different – value investors don't strive to be fully invested at all times; in fact value investors prefer to hold enough cash in the portfolio to allow them the flexibility to seize stocks as they become available at previously established attractive prices. Of course, if cash is being used to make a new investment in stocks, then that new investment has been determined to offer better risk/reward than one or more existing investments, which would then be sold to replenish cash.

Why as an investment manager it might seem easier to run with relative returns

In Chapter 10 I have included a table with estimates for how long each type of research activity might take for a single company – you will appreciate those estimates better after we discuss research and valuation processes in Chapters 4 and 5. But fundamentally there are two hurdles for an investment manager choosing to pursue absolute returns in technology stocks – 1) huge time commitment required for research, and 2) lack of industry expertise.

Why do your own equity research when you can just as easily follow (aka "chase") stock picks made by other respected investors like Warren Buffet, Seth Klarman, or David Einhorn? It is indeed quite tempting to go "research-lite", shifting the burden of research to other famed investors, who can then be conveniently blamed if things don't really work out in the end. Having outsourced the research function in this fashion, the investment manager can then focus on doing things he is really good at – i.e. mixing up such externally generated stock ideas in just the right proportions to beat the benchmark index. This seems to especially be the case with growth stocks like FB, AMZN, NFLX, GOOG, (aka "FANG") where all the copycat stock chasing leads to a run-up in expectations so high that companies no matter how fast they are growing or how profitable they are, would ultimately struggle to satisfy. It shouldn't be surprising then that the average investment manager struggles to beat benchmark index performance.

Of course this is probably not behavior that you should expect the average investment manager to admit, or even recognize, because it has become commonplace and ingrained across the industry. This is why I prefer to be value-biased, with a focus on absolute returns powered by independent equity research.

Institutional Investors Do Not Have an Information Advantage

If you are under the misperception that large institutional investors somehow get access to more information earlier than everyone else, then that is no longer true. Reg FD (Regulation Fair Disclosure) has forced companies to make sure their press releases and other presentations are made accessible to all investors at the same time. If a company hosts an analyst event, whether it's an earnings call, or other business update call or meeting, it can be followed real-time via webcast. It is unlawful for companies to provide privileged information to any outsider; so if you think "special" investors can get selective access to material updates from companies in advance of the common public, then that hasn't been true at least over the last decade. In other words, institutional investors really do not have an information advantage over individual investors or investment managers.

Think about this – a large proportion of major technology companies are either based in or have a significant presence in the Silicon Valley (California). Investors on the other hand are concentrated in financial centers – such as New York, London, and Hong Kong. How often do you think institutional investors get to meet with engineers and managers at the tech companies that they follow? Hardly if ever, except in controlled environments supervised and policed by the company's investor relations staff. In other words, institutional investors are more or less confined to the official bulletins provided by the companies specifically for the purpose of investor education. They have no real chance of digging behind the canned presentations to understand what might be happening in the real world. There is good reason for this. Most importantly, this is the best way for company managements to make sure they are following Reg FD as rigorously as they possibly can. Even if Reg FD were not in the way, tech companies understand their investors on average are not engineers and might not be tech savvy - this means investors wouldn't necessarily know how to interpret detail information they might receive from talking with a company engineer for example. Worse, they could misinterpret and/or misuse that information. All reasons to make sure institutional investors play within the sandbox of information provided to them along with the common public.

If institutional investors don't have an information advantage, then how are they supposed to come up with a deeper fundamental understanding that gives them an investment edge over other investors? If they can't develop an investment edge, then how will they outperform?

Value vs. Deep Value

When Benjamin Graham first introduced value investing, his focus was on estimating liquidation value of assets underlying a stock or a bond, with less importance placed on product or industry-specific dynamics as a source of potential future value. Today, Graham's original approach is sometimes referred to as "deep value" investing. Warren Buffet, Seth Klarman, and other practitioners, over time have expanded on Graham's original approach to include a broader range of companies, including what some might call "growth" companies, within the philosophy of value investing. The approach I discuss in this book builds on Buffet-style investing, with a focus on Technology stocks.

Absolute vs. Relative Returns Summary

The table on the next page summarizes the preceding discussion and provides a comparison of absolute vs. relative return strategies, for the benefit of the individual investor (or her investment manager).

Value investing as discussed throughout this book is an Absolute Return strategy, which is based at its core on fundamental analysis of companies and industries. Putting aside all semantics, I think the biggest problem with relative return strategies is that they are not based on fundamental analysis of companies or industries. Yet you will find a number of (if not most of) mutual fund and hedge fund managers aggressively market themselves as fundamentals-driven managers. Like I said, it may seem like the financial services industry thrives on keeping individual investors in a state of confusion.

	Absolute Returns	Relative Returns
Investment Focus	Protection and growth of dollar value of investment	Investment Performance at or better than chosen benchmark
Capital Preservation	Primary Focus	Secondary objective
Capital Growth	Primary Focus	Secondary objective
Investment Manager	Individual Investors and their Independent Investment Managers	Most Mutual Funds, Hedge Funds, ETFs, and other types of managers
Stock Selection	Driven by Fundamental Analysis of Company and Industry	Driven by assessment of how other investors might behave
Macro Analysis	Not a focus, but broader views can be incorporated	Varies, but usually is core to investment process
Investment Horizon	Longer Term, 2-to-5 years or more	Shorter Term, less than 1-year on average
Investment Style	Some form of Value Investing	Not Value Investing, but may still be labeled as "value" or "growth" funds

There is a way out for individual investors …

And it involves independent equity research, executed through a trusted independent investment manager. The next chapter is the longest chapter in the book, and it focuses on company analysis, a critical pillar of equity research.

Chapter 4 – RESEARCH PROCESS: COMPANY ANALYSIS

A View of Market Participants

Equity research focused on company and industry fundamentals is what differentiates investors from traders. Traders are typically less concerned about fundamentals, and more focused on technical indicators that capture short-term price movements of stocks. In the real world however, there is a continuum of market participants that range from longer-term investors at one end, to traders at the other end. The chart below illustrates this continuum.

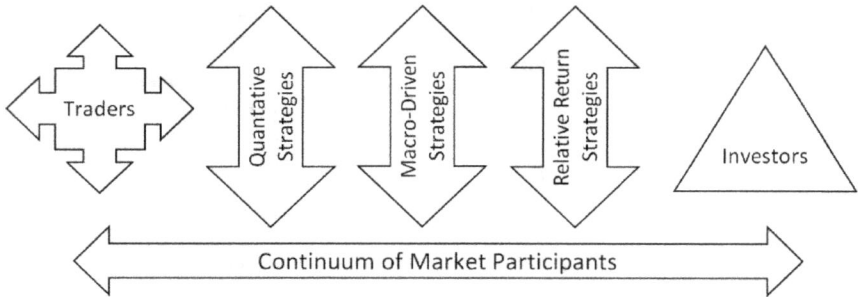

What's an Investment Thesis?

The next chart illustrates the relationship between research and trading for a longer-term investor. Research drives stock selection, and trading is performed to align ownership of individual stocks with the overall strategy established for an investment portfolio. Company and industry analysis drives the formulation of an investment thesis, which forms the basis for valuation analysis. *An investment thesis should capture the rationale for owning (or not owning, or shorting) a particular company's stock, an explicit and specific description of the risks involved, and valuation scenarios that provide guidelines for buying or selling that particular stock.*

Equity Research		Trading
Company Analysis	Valuation Analysis	Buy/Sell Discipline

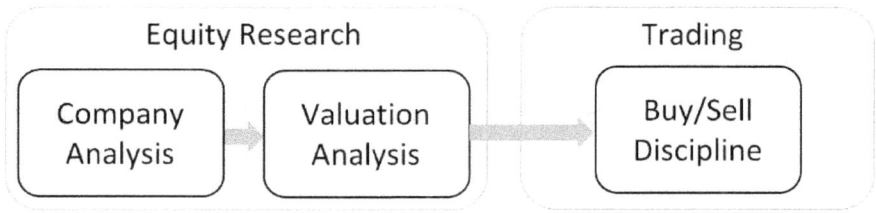

An investment thesis may also be referred to as a "stock pitch" or an "equity research report". Having a well analyzed and properly articulated investment thesis for a given stock, is a core part of being a fundamentals-driven longer-term investor.

In this chapter I will discuss different tools and techniques that I have used to analyze a company, with the ultimate goal of determining the investment thesis for its stock. The next chapter will focus on valuation analysis and buy/sell discipline.

Company Analysis

A number of activities are core to carrying out investment due diligence on a given stock for a given company. The chart below applies to public companies, but the core process would be similar for private companies as well. The chart captures different activities that are involved in analyzing a company's business, with a view to valuing its stock.

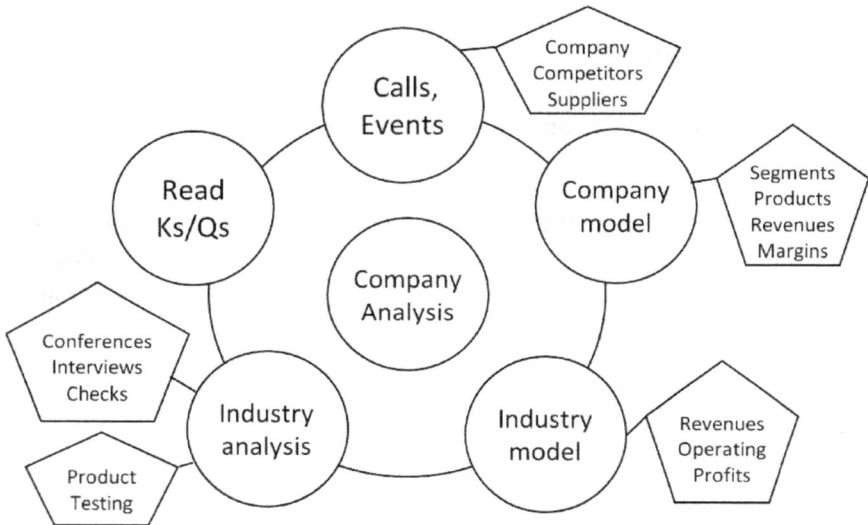

Calls, Events, Transcripts: I have found that the most effective way to get to know a company is to go through several of its most recent earnings calls – either listen to live or recorded calls, or read call transcripts. Usually reviewing the eight most recent transcripts provides a good starting point for forming an initial view of how a company is doing. If you want to be efficient with this process, it is helpful to record the various numbers provided by management over time, in a spreadsheet, which can later be reconciled with other inputs.

In addition to reviewing a given company's recent management commentary, you next have to review commentary provided by its key competitors, partners and suppliers, following a similar process for recording relevant metrics provided by managements of those companies.

10Ks, 10Qs, 8Ks, 20Fs: Reviewing a company's regulatory filings offers another view of its business. I have found it worthwhile paying attention to how management describes a company's strategy, its priorities, and its view of different challenges and risks inherent to its business. I have encountered many an investor that either hadn't read or misunderstood what management wrote in a company's quarterly or annual filings. Various tools are available to track changes from year to year in management's description of the business – such tools can be helpful, but I have not needed them. Either way, you still have to process several filings to grasp how a company might be changing or shifting focus.

In addition to management commentary, you will find a lot of quantitative information in such filings, and a lot of it needs to be captured in the company model that you will build. This includes primarily segment details, various accounting reconciliations (e.g. balance sheet and cash flow) that are needed to make complete sense of the model, details related to ownership interests in various types of assets (e.g. other businesses, bonds, other financial instruments), obligations related to different types of leases or guarantees, purchase contracts, etc.

Company Model

Building a financial model for a given company is comprised of a number of activities, which I have grouped into distinct categories in the chart below. Categories shaded in blue would be considered to represent relatively straightforward or largely mechanical activities with few unknowns. Categories shaded orange/red involve a lot of judgment, and also generate the most value from building a company model.

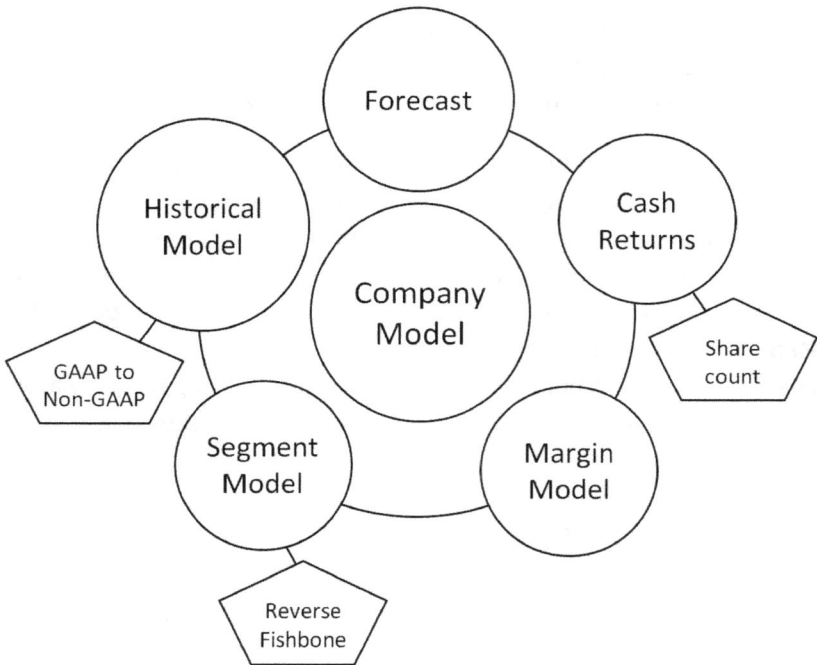

Historical Model

There are three ways to build a historical model: 1) build a model from scratch, 2) download a model from a data service like Sentieo, and build on it, or 3) start from a good sellside model provided by your friendly equity sales person, and build on it.

I have built a number of models from scratch, with the most difficult one of them being a model for Samsung Electronics – more on that later.

Some companies are kind enough to provide starter models on their websites – TSMC is one such company, among very few in the technology space, to make a great effort to provide model information to investors proactively. In the absence of such a high quality starter model, you will need to build one in Excel manually. As mentioned earlier, you will want to work backwards in time, starting with the most recent period, and updating the model one quarter at a time going back in history, referring to publicly available filings from the company (10K/10Q). This is a manual and tedious process, but at least in the end you will have a high quality model that you can be confident represents facts communicated by the company.

Starter models can be downloaded in various formats from services like Sentieo or Factset. In each case however, there is significant additional effort involved in restructuring the model to match the company's reporting format, as well as auditing data to ensure data quality issues don't crop up later.

Using a good sellside model would trump both the above methods, the keyword being "good". The less you have to spot check, the faster you can progress to the next step, which is to build a segment model.

Segment Model - Reverse Fishbone Analysis

To keep the analysis focused, efficient, and results-oriented, I have found it effective to work backwards from the company's top level revenues and profits to determine what its key drivers are. This type of analysis is sometimes called "reverse fishbone" analysis, because you will be starting with a smaller number of variables, progressively building out next layers of detail to ultimately pinpoint which products, technologies, businesses or segments are the most important in creating value for shareholders.

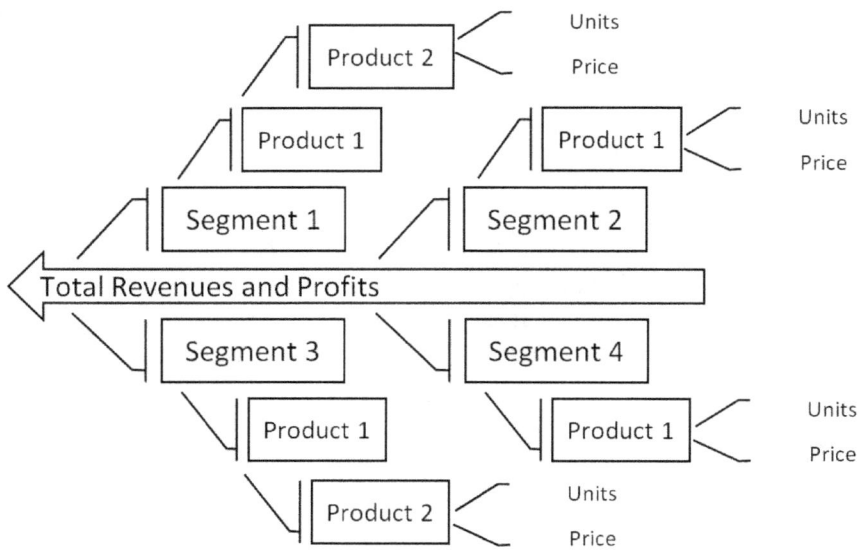

The chart below shows a detail quarterly build-up by storage configuration for iPhone shipments over a roughly two year period.

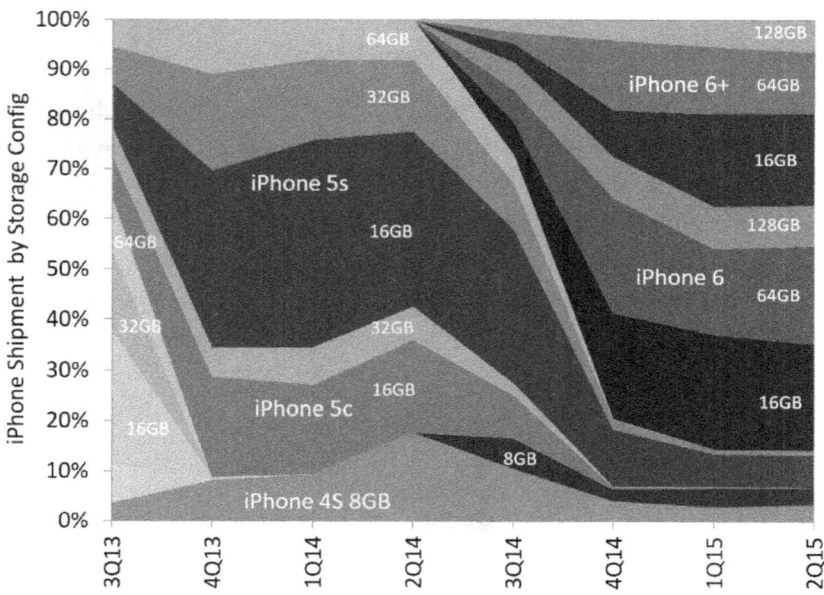

The chart below shows another example of such analysis for IBM. The segment characterizations shown below are different from IBM's officially reported segments, but based on information presented by management during earnings calls and other presentations.

	CY13	CY14	CY15	CY16E	CY17E	CY18E
% of Revs						
Strategic Imperatives	22%	27%	35%	40%	45%	50%
Big data/analytics	16%	18%	22%			
Cloud	4%	8%	13%			
As a Service	2%	3%	6%			
Mobile						
Social						
Core	65%	62%	55%	50%	45%	40%
Hardware	13%	11%	9%	10%	10%	10%
YoY Growth (%)	**-4%**	**-6%**	**-12%**	**-1%**	**1%**	**1%**
Strategic Imperatives		16%	16%	13%	12%	12%
Big data/analytics		7%	6%			
Cloud		60%	57%			
As a Service		80%	51%			
Mobile			250%			
Social			21%			
Core		-10%	-21%	-10%	-8%	-10%
Hardware	-19%	-19%	-27%	1%	1%	1%

Recasting the company's business in this fashion draws attention to the Strategic Imperatives segment, which is growing rapidly, and is likely to become a bigger driver of overall company value going forward. It also raises the question of why management isn't changing its segment reporting to be consistent with how it's telling the company's strategic story.

3-Statement Company Financial Model

I build company models most commonly comprising of three interconnected financial statements – income statement, balance sheet, and cash flow, supported by one or more "bottom up" models for revenues, margins, etc. This is commonly referred to as a "working model", because changes made in any of the financial statements propagate throughout the entire model. When starting out covering new companies, I have found it useful to have annual data built out going back as far as possible/available. I have typically started out building historical quarterly data for three years. Once a functional model is ready, it can always be extended to include more historical data over time.

Company models can be built from scratch, using company filings usually made available on company websites in their investor relations sections. If using this approach it is more efficient to work backwards, i.e. start from the most recent period, and then progressively work backwards in time to build out the historical model. Working backwards in time helps ensure you are using the most current information first, and avoids rework due to restatements that companies tend to issue occasionally (some companies more than others). An alternative to building company models from scratch is to start from either a well-reputed sellside model, or excel models that you can download from providers like MorningStar, Factset, or Sentieo. After downloading models from an automated service like Factset or Sentieo, you are faced with the additional task of restructuring the model to make sure that 1) it matches the company's reporting format, and 2) data quality of the model is acceptable.

Once the historical model has been built, the next step is to set up a framework for forecasting. "Top-down" forecasting is done at the financial statement level, usually starting with the income statement. Bottom-up forecasting on the other hand, is done starting from the segment or product level, such that an aggregation of segment revenues and profits drives the income statement. For top-down forecasting to work properly, appropriate linkages and formulas connecting the income statement, balance sheet and cash flow statement need to be put in place. The goal of this activity quite simply is for income statement assumptions and forecasts to translate into cash flow forecasts, which ultimately help with valuation.

Here are some best practices that I have followed for modeling. The specific details in this section have been written to be a reminder for me to build models with a consistent approach, rather than to serve as specific advice for other analysts. In that regard, this section is not written to be any sort of a primer for building models. While no one knows what the future holds, assumptions about the future have to be made nevertheless while assessing future value of a business. The key here I think is to use some guidelines or rules of thumb based on the particular company or business, such that forecasts are sensible rather than perfect.

Income Statement

Build out GAAP (Generally Accepted Accounting Principles) and non-GAAP reconciliations for each line item as applicable. There are several reasons why companies might choose to deviate from standard GAAP reporting, and provide various forms of non-GAAP representations of their performance. Usually it comes down to one or more of the following elements:

Heavy use of stock-based compensation, which some companies view as a non-cash expense. I as well as others have done work showing that over the longer term, reported stock-option compensation expense actually approximates cash flow to a company's employees. So ignoring stock-based comp completely may not be prudent for an investor, given that it does represent an important use of cash, to retain (and enrich) employees. It is often the case that young companies, that have just executed an IPO, carry higher levels of stock-comp expense, which they exclude when reporting non-GAAP earnings. Unfortunately however, many companies continue to exclude stock-comp expense several years after IPO, and tracking non-GAAP EPS becomes a widely adopted metric for measuring performance of such companies. This can work for companies that continue to grow at a fast pace, and trade at a premium. However, when growth slows, investors would have one more thing to be worried about – valuation measured off non-GAAP EPS estimates. Companies like Cavium (NASDAQ: CAVM) and Inphi (NASDAQ: IPHI) would fall into this category of high-growth, premium-valued businesses that trade primarily off non-GAAP EPS.

M&A activity introduces "one-time" or extraordinary items that may not be directly relevant to the company's core business. Mergers and acquisitions trigger a flurry of accounting changes that generate a number of "one-time" charges which actually aren't one-time in that they persist for several quarters if not years after the M&A has been completed. Examples of such charges would be amortization of acquired intangibles, inventory step-up, litigation charges, etc.

Licensing or other business models translate into deviations between actual vs. reported business activity. Whenever there is a significant structural difference between the timing of revenues and the timing of related cash flows, a company may consider introducing a non-GAAP measure of progress, for revenues, costs, or both.

This is why having a model that carefully disaggregates the different income statement items, and provides an easily readable GAAP to non-GAAP reconcilation, is valuable. See the chart below.

Income Statement			2012	
	DecQ	MarQ	JunQ	SepQ
R&D - GAAP	25.0	26.0	30.0	28.0
Acquisition Related Costs	(0.5)			
Equity Compensation Expense	(1.0)	(2.0)	(2.0)	(2.1)
R&D - Non-GAAP	23.5	24.0	28.0	25.9
as % of Sales	10.7%	11.0%	12.0%	10.8%
SG&A - GAAP	29.3	32.6	35.6	35.0
Acquisition Related Costs				
Equity Compensation Expense	(3.0)	(3.1)	(5.0)	(5.0)
Litigation Related	1.0			
SG&A - Non-GAAP	27.3	29.5	30.6	30.0
as % of Sales	12.4%	13.5%	13.1%	12.5%
Restructuring & Other - Non-GAAP	-	-	-	-
as % of Sales	0.0%	0.0%	0.0%	0.0%
OpEx - Non-GAAP	50.8	53.6	58.5	55.9
as % of Sales	23.1%	24.5%	25.1%	23.3%

Unfortunately, modern financial data services like Factset or Sentieo do not provide much help when it comes to building such GAAP to non-GAAP reconcilation in the model. In fact, even company filings like 10Ks or 10Qs often omit such data, and the analyst is left to her own determination to plow through historical earnings presentations or press releases to extract reconciliatory data provided by companies. Of all the companies I have seen, I think SanDisk probably did the best job of providing a single page reconciliation table providing all the details in an easily readable format. There are a few companies that probably like to play games with analysts, by leaving out items like "tax effect of stock-based comp" or "tax effect of extraordinary expenses", assuming that analysts would find a way to plug such estimates.

Forecasting Revenues

This is probably the most important part of the analysis that determines what a company is worth or will be worth over time. Top-down forecasting can be done by setting quarterly revenue growth rates, usually based on an assumed seasonality in revenue patterns based on historical performance. Annual revenue growth rates should be consistent with company guidance, to the extent it has been provided. Once a baseline top-down revenue forecast has been programmed into the model, subsequent refining is best done with the help of a "bottom-up" or segment model.

A bottom-up model is used to capture specific assumptions or expectations from individual business segments or product lines, as we discussed in reverse fishbone analysis. Annual growth rates and seasonality assumptions can be applied to each business segment for a more realistic representation of company fundamentals. Qualitative and quantitative analysis of the company and applicable industries can be leveraged to drive further refinement in bottom up assumptions, by factoring in 1) product cycles, 2) industry dynamics, 3) market share changes, 4) price changes, 5) contract renewals, 6) geographical dynamics, 7) product mix changes, and a number of other variables.

Through a process of iteratively adjusting top-down and bottom-up assumptions, the goal is to come up with a reasonably robust forecast that takes into account the best information you have about the company's fundamentals. It is helpful to benchmark your forecasts relative to available data about consensus forecasts, to be aware of major deviations in your model relative to the market consensus, and explicitly document the rationale for such deviations if you decide that they deserve to prevail.

Forecasting Gross Margins

Armed with revenue forecasts, the next step is to estimate gross margins. Again the first step is to incorporate company guidance on a top-down basis, and apply other history-based forecasting techniques to come up with baseline estimates. Next your bottom-up model needs to be enhanced to incorporate segment-level gross margin estimates. This might be easier to do for software companies that don't have much in the way of fixed costs, but harder to do for heavily manufacturing-oriented businesses, such as semiconductor companies.

Assuming that you have already factored in the effect of pricing while forecasting revenues, the incremental effort to estimate gross margins involves estimating costs. For manufacturing businesses, you have to think about different types of costs, including depreciation, factory startup costs, under-utilization charges, etc. If you have already modeled product mix (mix of products with different revenues and margins), then it will be easier to estimate segment margins.

As with everything else in modeling, how much detail you need to build depends on where you think non-consensus insights might be hidden. The goal is not to build a perfect model of the company, but rather to identify potential sources of mispricing for the stock. If you lose sight of this and just mechanically keep digging to build out more detail, then you might end up with a good-looking model that doesn't necessarily provide a lot of investment insight. Knowing where to dig is very important, and this is why you have to get out of your office and talk to industry experts.

Other Items of Note

Unless management has provided other specific guidance, I typically forecast OpEx to grow at half the rate of revenue growth.

Interest income/expense items should be linked to cash/debt balances and interest rates estimates on the Balance Sheet.

Sharecount should include buyback assumptions, as well as dilution from convertible debt. For this purpose, it is useful to model both basic and diluted shares, GAAP and non-GAAP.

Analyze Use of Cash

The next chart depicts four broad categories of use of cash that a company has to allocate properly. Cash needed to run the business falls in the "Working and Growth Capital" bucket, which includes portions of OpEx, working capital, and CapEx. With excess cash that is left over and generated from running the business, management needs to allocate cash across M&A, cash returns (buybacks and dividends) or other investments. This is not as easy as it might look, as use of cash obviously must be consistent with the company's stated strategy.

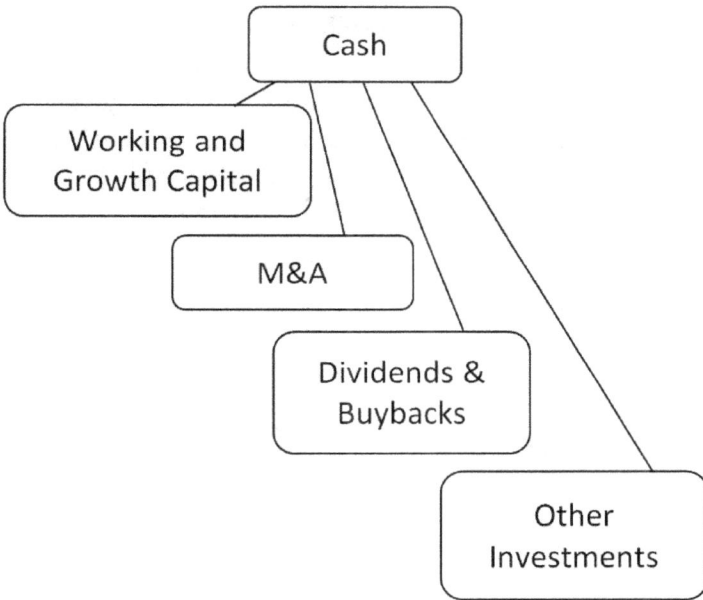

In fact analyzing use of cash can provide clues into how the company is thinking about its business strategy, and whether it thinks M&A is important for delivering future growth. Once investors get the sense that cash is just piling up and not being put to appropriate use, you will start to see different types of activism crop up, with the objective of releasing some or all of that excess cash back to shareholders, who can then allocate that cash potentially toward other investments. In fact Warren Buffet has famously taken this concept all the way to the point where he ends up owning entire businesses, relieving management of the need to worry about appropriate allocation of cash. As we will discuss in the next chapter on valuation, this is also why I think cash on the balance sheet does not command much in terms of valuation credit when it comes to assessing upside scenarios, but certainly provides downside protection for intrinsic value.

Before analyzing use of cash, it may be worthwhile to first check where the company's cash is located and/or generated. For a number of technology companies like Apple for example, most of the cash from operations is generated and located overseas, i.e. outside the U.S. Overseas cash cannot be directly used for share repurchases or for paying dividends, until it is first repatriated back to the U.S., a process that involves paying a significant amount of taxes to the U.S. government. You may find that to sustain its cash return commitments, a company will need to raise debt, sometimes a lot of it. Knowing this beforehand can properly balance what you model for share repurchases or dividend growth in your forecasts.

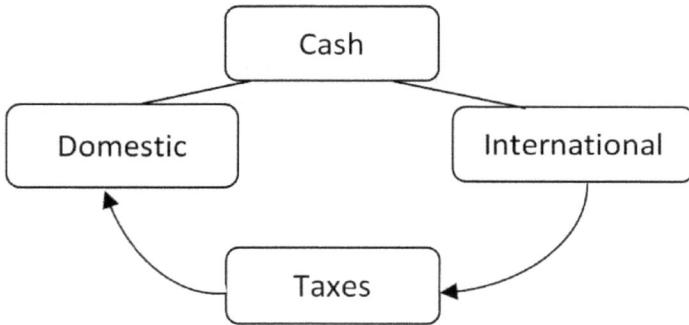

```
                        ┌──────────┐
                        │   Cash   │
                        └──────────┘
        ┌────────────┐              ┌───────────────┐
        │  Domestic  │              │ International  │
        └────────────┘              └───────────────┘
                        ┌──────────┐
                        │  Taxes   │
                        └──────────┘
```

CapEx

For businesses that require heavy CapEx investments, it is worthwhile forming a good understanding of the longer-term CapEx outlay. Higher the CapEx, lower the free cash flow (FCF). The next chart shows my CapEx intensity estimates for TSMC, the largest contract manufacturer of semiconductor chips. CapEx intensity is calculated as CapEx divided by

76

revenues, and provides one framework to think about a company's CapEx commitments relative to its overall manufacturing cost structure.

CapEx Intensity

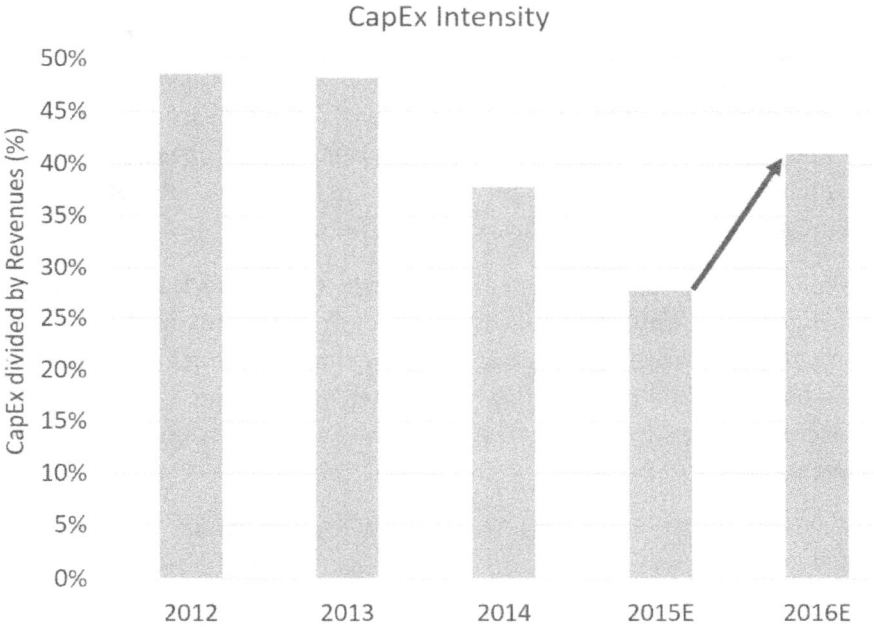

TSMC for example has generated gross margins in the 45%-to-50% range for a long time, but has also spent CapEx at a similar level. If almost every dollar of gross profit is committed toward CapEx, then how is the company funding its OpEx and dividends? Something to think about …

CapEx eventually flows through the income statement in the form of depreciation, and the question is how long does it take for that to happen. Unless a company's business model is structurally changing, or there is some sort of accounting effect in play, it is fair to expect that over the long term a company's CapEx would be comparable to its Depreciation to ensure that productive assets are being added to the asset base approximately at the same rate as they are getting consumed or obsoleted.

Forecasting Dividends & Buybacks

I have learnt that forecasting dividends and buybacks explicitly is helpful to form a good understanding of a company's cash return potential, and avoid over-estimating such gains. Forecasting dividends is straightforward, and can be done on a total dollar amount basis or per share basis.

For estimating the effect of buybacks, a few additional assumptions need to be made. First, having historical data for basic shares is useful, as it can be used to estimate a baseline rate of growth for the basic sharecount. Any buybacks which would have the effect of lowering sharecount, would be offset by such intrinsic upward drift in sharecount.

Next you need to estimate cash available for buybacks. As discussed previously, its important to estimate cash available in the U.S. for companies domiciled in the U.S., as this will be some fraction of the total cash balance. Explicitly factoring in expected debt issuances or refinancing is useful to get a good idea of the total cash available for buybacks in each forecast period.

Finally you need to come up with a working assumption for the company's share price progression over future periods. For this purpose, assuming share prices will be higher would actually lead to a more conservative estimate of the buyback benefit.

Armed with these assumptions, now you can go ahead and calculate the net reduction in sharecount due to explicitly modeled buybacks in future periods.

ROIC Analysis: DRAM Case Study

The next chart illustrates the process of analyzing Return on Invested Capital (ROIC) for an investment related to new DRAM memory manufacturing capacity. The purpose of such analysis is to determine whether new investment in a project is likely to generate adequate returns.

The first step is to determine what the period and the hurdle rate for the investment would be. Since semiconductor manufacturing equipment has historically been depreciated over 5 years, the example uses a 5 year period, and assumes a hurdle rate of 10%.

In Year 0, an investment of $500m is made to install 10K WSPM (wafer starts per month) of new manufacturing capacity for DRAM memory chips. Cash inflows in Years 1 to 5 are assumed to be identical for simplicity, at $132m each. The rest of the detail underneath the discounted cash flow portion at the top, is used to determine what DRAM market prices (ASP per GB needed) would need to be in order to support the ROIC calculation.

If you ignore the technical jargon in the calculations, basically what this analysis is telling you is that if you don't think DRAM prices can be at least $6.51 per GB on average for the next 5 years, then you don't have a good chance of generating your target ROIC of 10%.

	Year 0	Year 1	Year 2	Year 3	Year 4	Year 5
Free Cash flow ($, m)	-500	132	132	132	132	132
NPV	0					
IRR	10%					

Economics of Incremental Capacity

Size of increment (WSPM)	10,000
Cost of increment ($, m)	500
Wafer processing cost per wafer ($)	1,300
Gross die per wafer (4Gb die)	1,400
Yield rate	90%
Good die per wafer (4Gb die)	1,260
DRAM output (GB) per wafer	630
DRAM output per year (GB, m)	76
Wafer Processing Cost per GB	2.06
Back-end processing cost per GB	0.80
Manufacturing Cost per GB	2.86
OpEx per GB	1.91
Total Cost per GB	**4.77**
EBIT per GB needed ($)	1.75
ASP per GB needed	**6.51**

Industry Analysis

"Insanity: doing the same thing over and over again and expecting different results" – Albert Einstein

Generating better investment results requires following a different process than the one followed by the average investor. A big part of where I consciously did things differently often came down to industry analysis. Attending conferences and interviewing industry experts is something many investors do, but depending on how this process is executed, the outcomes can be wildly different.

The chart below shows the industry conferences that I attended or tracked. If you attend a conference, but don't have a plan for who to talk to and what to ask, then you are not going to be very productive – at least not in a way that is different from the average investor. Similarly, if in every one of your meetings you are running into other investors who are asking the same questions, then again your output from the conference isn't going to look much different from that of your competitors.

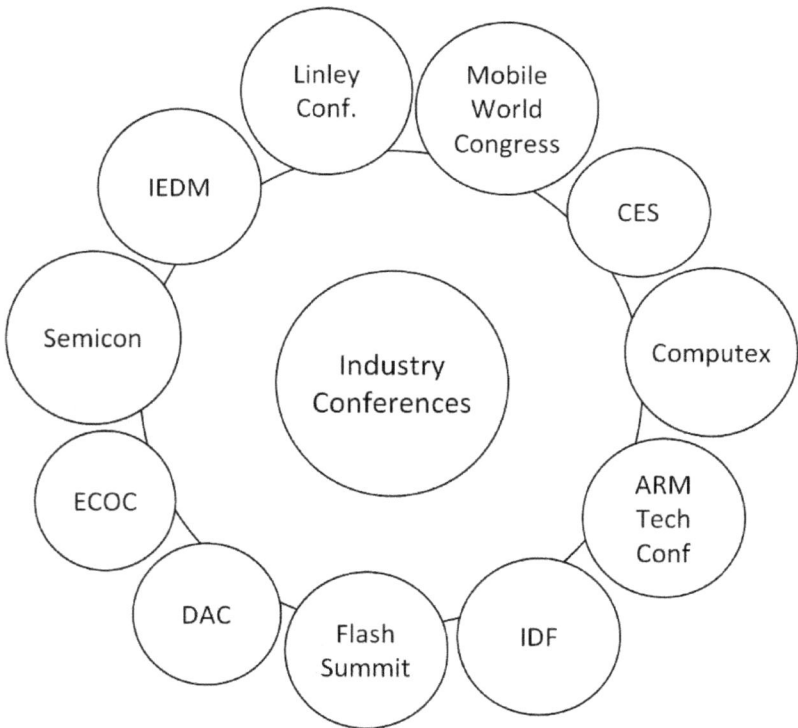

Fact is that following a company or an industry is a continuous and time-consuming process, one that I think the average generalist investor (or generalist turned specialist investor) is unsuited for, largely by definition – because she is going to be focused on many companies across many industries, and is unlikely to be able to commit sufficient time or resources to a single industry. While she would still generate copious amounts of research notes from all the conferences she attends, she may not be able to fully internalize all of it. She will try has hard as she can to process the spoken or written word in the presentations, missing subtle undertones, politics, and changes brewing underneath the surface. And she can hardly be blamed for it, because she wasn't adequately qualified for the job in the first place.

Planning for such conferences includes identifying which investment themes you are going to focus on, which attendees are likely to provide insight, and what specific questions you are going to ask. In addition to the "usual" meetings, you are looking for lesser known companies that may be more inclined to talk with you, particularly if they think they can learn something from you.

Visiting showfloor exhibit booths can be enormously valuable if you can find the right people to talk to, and have the right questions to ask. I have learnt that asking questions that focus on strategic topics highly relevant to the other person tends to generate the most meaningful discussion. Clearly, to know what is strategic, you need to do your homework ahead of time. I have witnessed many an investor boldly (and insensitively) asking questions that are either inappropriate or offensive to the other person. In many cases this isn't an inadvertent mistake, but rather a strategy to ask such questions to guage the other person's reaction. Needless to say such an approach isn't designed for, nor is it successful at building trust-based relationships.

Testing new products and watching product demo presentations hosted by booth personnel can be educational, insightful, and entertaining. For me this has certainly been a great way to learn about new technologies and capabilities first hand, rather than reading about them second hand in blogs. In addition to such industry conferences, analyst days hosted by individual companies are also a huge resource that should not be underestimated, as a starting point for analysis.

Case Study – Memory Industry Analysis

In order to form a strong understanding of the DRAM and NAND memory industries, I spent a lot of time in South Korea, where two of the world's largest memory makers are based – Samsung Electronics and SK hynix. Understanding what motivates them, what challenges they face, and how they see the rest of the world including their customers and competitors was core to understanding how the industry functioned. I took every chance I got to attend presentations given by senior management at these companies, in forums around the world. I engaged with mid-senior managers to understand their view of the business, and where there were potential disconnects within their organizations. None of this was easy because I started with virtually zero contacts at either of these companies. The one thing that I uniquely brought to the table was my industry experience, which formed a basis for my questions, and proved to be helpful in connecting with professionals at these companies.

You can build all the models you want, but the models are not going to magically answer all the questions you have – you cannot create insight out of thin air by building models. I complemented my engagements with Samsung and SK hynix with additional relationships with memory industry experts based in Taiwan and in the U.S. Collectively, I put in place a robust framework of industry relationships to test my assumptions and inputs that I was feeding into my models. After doing all of this, it is still possible to be wrong, particularly in the short-term, but at least you have a basis for refining your assumptions and figuring out if you have a chance to be right longer term.

Industry Model

Continuing with the memory industry case study, I learnt it was fashionable among memory industry watchers to have and constantly refer to an industry supply/demand model. So I built a supply/demand model, from scratch. I quickly realized that the model could at most help determine sensitivities of different types of changes – e.g. supply shock or demand shock, on the overall S/D balance, but wouldn't be capable of providing conclusive insight about whether the industry would be over-supplied or under-supplied in the short-term. There was also no way for the model to take into account inventory levels in the supply chain, because none of the supply chain participants reported their inventories. Without incorporating inventories, which none of the industry models were capable of, it was impossible to have a perfect view of supply/demand in the short-term.

Unless you are building an industry model purely to gain a historical understanding of industry dynamics, this is a common problem you will encounter across any industry model. I find industry models most useful for the following types of activities:

1) Understanding industry structure, and competitive dynamics by using a framework like the Hefindahl-Hirschman Index (HHI)
2) Determining the size and distribution of industry profit pools
3) Determine the impact of a product cycle
4) Understand growth rates across different sub-segments of the market
5) Understand the impact of upcoming new product categories

Building an industry model for any industry is a giant task, not to be undertaken without a good understanding of how it can be leveraged for investment gains. I have personally built such industry models for memory (DRAM/NAND/NOR), microprocessors, graphics processors, mobile devices, semiconductor capital equipment, and display panels, and each model proved to be extremely valuable in making investment calls across different slices of the technology industry.

Working with Imperfect Information

As it is probably becoming clear to you, there are usually no short-cuts in forming your investment thesis. If you do stumble upon a short-cut, it is worth asking yourself if information that you came across could be considered material non-public information (MNPI). Using MNPI (aka "insider information") to make investments is illegal. If by law you are not allowed to have specific, clear-cut, definitive pieces of information in advance of it becoming public knowledge, then by definition you are operating on imperfect information in the interim, as you make investment decisions.

If trained properly, the human brain can serve as a powerful filter and synthesizer of discrete pieces of information. As scientists researching machine learning and artificial intelligence are finding out, depth and breadth of the data that a machine can absorb, store, and process, drives its ability to make actionable predictions. Clearly, a brain exposed to years of insight in the technology space, through industry training across multiple disciplines, will be more adept at processing technology data points, as compared to a brain that has been exposed only to say, financial data. Using my favorite example of a medical doctor, the more experience a doctor has in terms of the range of conditions he has analyzed and cured, the better his brain will be at judging problems that may not be fully represented in observable symptoms.

Avoiding Modeling Pitfalls and Common Errors

A model will largely show you what you want to see – in other words, a model itself will not automatically generate investment insights. A model can be used to quantify or refine insights that you have previously gathered, and measure the relationships between different variables connected to your thesis. Building precise models is difficult if not impossible because available information is frequently far from perfect. It is important not to get carried away by models, and lose sight of the real world. In that sense, identifying a set of checks for a model upfront can help eliminate big modeling problems quickly, and bring the model to a state of refinement that makes it usable and dependable.

Below I am describing a few techniques that I have followed, and that I believe are very easy to follow; yet I routinely come across analyses that would have hugely benefitted from application of these simple techniques.

Reconciling Annual Aggregations with Quarterly Data: The idea here is to keep your model consistent with itself – that shouldn't be too much to ask. Sum up your quarterly data for one year, and compare the total with what your model is calculating under the column for annual aggregations. This can be performed as a visual check, or can be implemented within an Excel model to flag an error when not satisfied. Errors arise when models have been subject to a mix of top-down and bottom-up forecasting, and the analyst has forgotten which portions were forecasted which way.

Checking Formula Extensions: Models are often extended to cover more periods in the future, or as time passes by, and the models need to be updated to include current data. The process of extending a model often involves copy-pasting formulae from prior periods into future periods. As simple as that sounds, it is easy to introduce errors while extending models, by linking the wrong elements in a formula. This must be checked explicitly to ensure no errors have been introduced.

Right-Sizing Models and Forecasts: When forecasting market growth for a product or service, it is possible to get carried away by company or industry commentary, and come up with estimates that defy real world constraints. One way to make sure models remain realistic is to use multiple independent frameworks to estimate the future trajectory, using checkpoints comprised of data known with relatively higher confidence.

Case Study: IBM

The charts below illustrate my approach to industry analysis. Understanding the players, their value propositions, and how they deliver it, is important to forming a base on which to build your investment thesis. Without such a base, with concrete interpretations and assumptions about the industry, it is easy to be lost in a sea of company-specific "Kool-Aid" designed to brainwash investors into believing that the company they are reading about is the greatest of them all. Again I like to use a visual approach to lay down the functional blocks and their inter-relationships. I have found such drawings useful in testing my understanding with industry experts, before a lot of numbers are committed to the model.

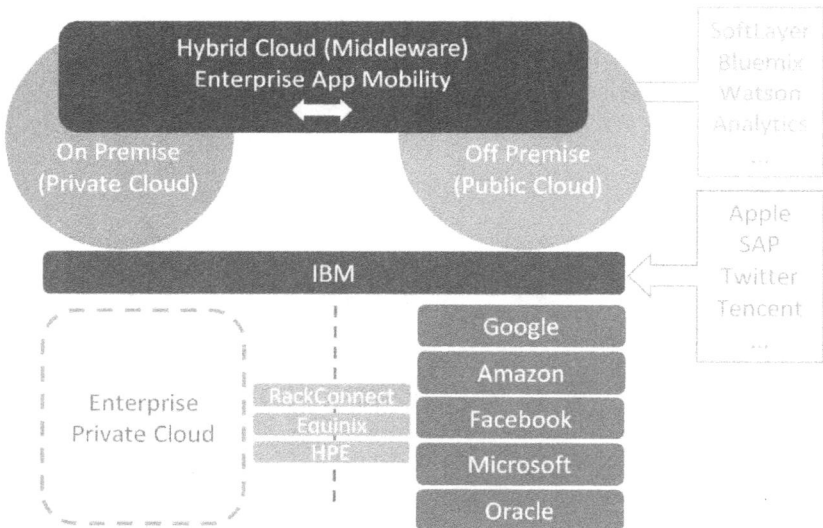

The chart above captures the concept of IBM's "Hybrid Cloud", and compares it with what IBM's Cloud competitors are doing. There is a lot of information packed into this chart, and this is how I like to build my understanding of a company or an industry, piece by piece. The chart can be updated or enhanced over time as information changes, or important new information becomes available.

The next chart illustrates IBM's various Cloud Service offerings, and compares how IBM's value proposition stacks up with that of its competitors. A quick glance at the chart suggests IBM is in a strong position to capture the most value as Enterprises make the transition to the Cloud. The chart also suggests that the "Infrastructure as a Service" (IaaS) is likely to be commoditized as a number of large players step up their Cloud offerings using lower-cost standardized hardware that will increasingly become available going forward.

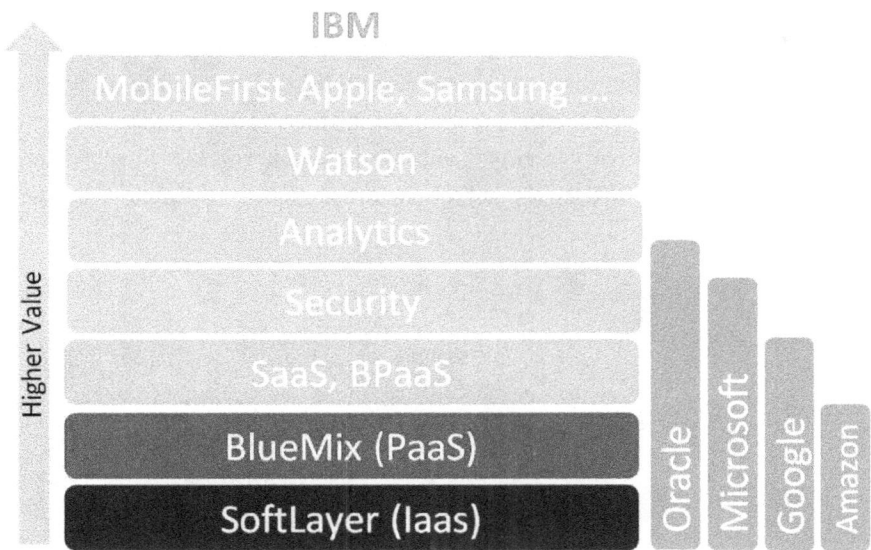

Next Step – Valuation

Putting together frameworks to solidify your understanding of the company and the industry is a stepping stone toward the goal of estimating intrinsic value of a stock. In the next chapter I describe a process for scenario analysis, which generates a range of estimates for intrinsic value, along with an indication of whether your analysis has led you to be bullish or bearish on a stock, a bias that may hold commercial value. As you might have guessed, the process of forecasting isn't done until after you carry out scenario analysis.

Chapter 5 – RESEARCH PROCESS: VALUATION ANALYSIS

Probably the most important thing to recognize upfront about valuation is that it is an art, not a science. I have had many smart technology professionals come up to me to offer me lessons on company valuation, through application of differential calculus, among other things. One mistake people make is that they think a company's intrinsic value is some fixed deterministic number that they can reliably reference or count on – unfortunately in valuation there's nothing further from the truth. Intrinsic value of a company is at best a range, which in theory changes with an investor's perception of a company's longer-term fundamentals - for technology companies, intrinsic value can swing meaningfully as various new developments impact business fundamentals, sometimes quickly. Yet in an online search for "intrinsic value" you will readily find a lot of quantitative models and tools, which promise a deterministic valuation for a given company.

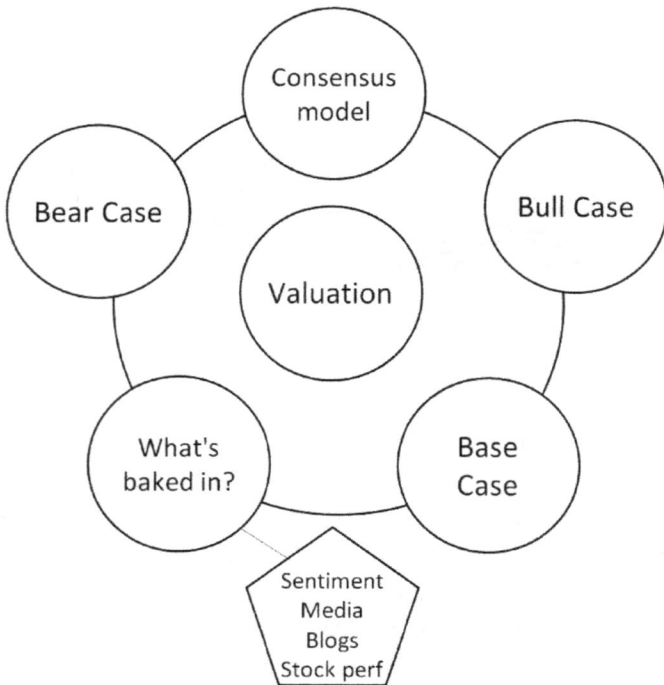

I have used scenario analysis, which theorizes a "Bull Case" scenario, a "Bear Case" scenario, and a "Base Case" or most likely scenario, along with potentially other intermediate scenarios, to form a range of fundamentals-driven outcomes for a company's business. Such scenario analysis can then be processed with different valuation frameworks to come up with a target intrinsic value range for an investment thesis.

Scenario Analysis

This is the most important and potentially value generating portion of analyzing a company model. The first step is to set the model to arrive at sellside consensus revenues and EPS, to estimate what bottom up assumptions are baked into sellside consensus thinking. The next step is to create Bull Case and Bear Case scenarios, to stretch bottom up assumptions in either direction, and determine how the company model looks in each of those scenarios. The last step is to create a Base Case model, which represents the most likely scenario in your mind, based on all the qualitative and quantitative industry and product analysis work that you have done. Each of these four scenarios should be saved as separate models for easy comparison. To determine if your scenario analysis indicates a bullish, bearish or neutral setup for the stock, you have to first determine what's baked into the stock price.

What's Baked into the Price?

In my process this is a critical piece of valuation analysis that I think is probably missed by the average investor, including professional and non-professional investors. The goal here is to form a perspective on what investors with an active position (long or short) in the stock are expecting in aggregate in terms of revenues, earnings, or other fundamentals. As with the rest of the investing process, this is not an exact science by any means.

The first thing to do here is to figure out what valuation metric the stock predominantly trades on – P/E NTM (aka Forward P/E), EV/S TTM, P/B, EV/FCF, etc. I have found that investors tend to use P/E NTM as the most common valuation metric for companies that have demonstrated EPS generation consistently. For companies that are unable to deliver EPS consistently, investors may resort to EV/S TTM, P/B or EV/FCF as valuation metrics.

The next step is to estimate the valuation level that investors have historically most commonly paid for the stock. For me this is usually a visual exercise, cycling through different periods of recent history to see if there is a significant pattern of consistent valuation around a certain level of P/E NTM for example, if that's the metric chosen in the first step.

The final step is to apply the historical valuation level to the current stock price to estimate what level of fundamentals investors are really expecting, i.e. paying for. The key insight here is that investors might be paying for a level of EPS that is higher or lower than that projected by the sellside consensus, and this will have an impact on whether you should buy, sell or do nothing with the stock.

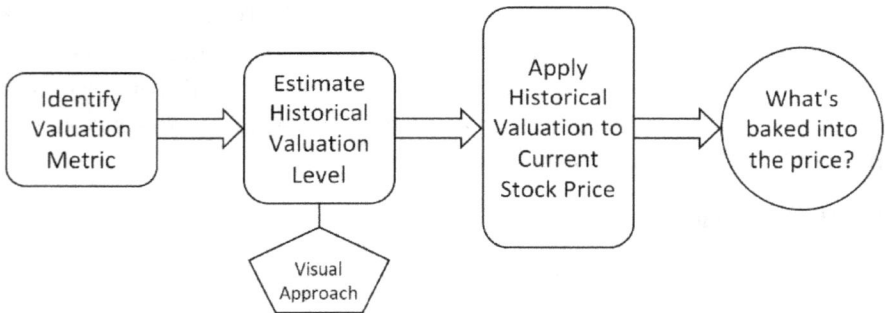

Valuation – A Visual Approach

I have learnt to appreciate that it is not always possible to write down a mathematical formula for every single variable that needs to be estimated. Valuation is no exception. There is a healthy element of "art" involved in equity research, especially when it comes to valuation. I like to take a more visual approach (aka eye-balling) to valuation. The charts below illustrate what I mean. Estimating with some confidence the historical valuation multiple that investors have consistently paid for a stock is important, because it informs what the stock would most likely be worth in the future when valued off potentially superior (or worse) fundamentals. It can also suggest whether investor expectations are elevated or depressed. Next-twelve-month (NTM) Price-to-earnings (P/E) is a valuation metric that I tend to use most often, but have also used other metrics like Enterprise Value to Sales Trailing Twelve Month (EV/S TTM), Enterprise Value to Free Cash Flow (EV/FCF), and Price to Book (P/B).

If you look at the chart for Micron (MU) below, my inference is that in recent periods MU has historically most often traded at P/E NTM of ~10x.

MU P/E NTM

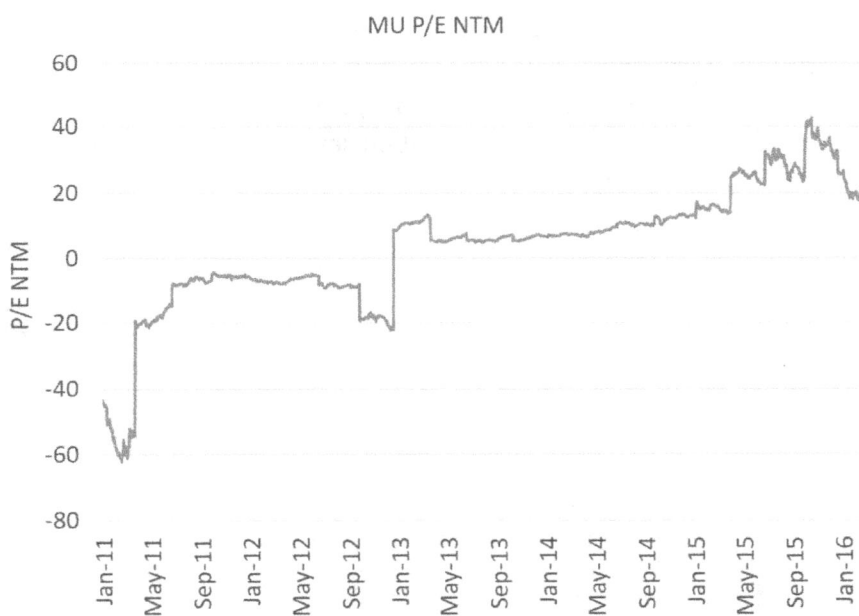

If the stock's current P/E is higher than its historical average level, then investors are potentially expecting a higher level of performance from the company, than that implied by the sellside consensus. For example, as of this writing, MU was trading at P/E NTM of ~20x. This would seem to suggest that holders of the stock (net of short sellers) were collectively expecting the company to deliver nearly 2x the level EPS estimated by sellside consensus over the next twelve months. This could be because buyside investors were taking a longer-term view of the stock, and paying a ~10x P/E for EPS that could potentially be generated 12-to-24 months out in the future. It could also be that following multiple disappointing quarters, the valuation metric shifted from P/E NTM to something else, like P/B.

Likewise, in the AAPL chart below, my inference is that AAPL had historically most often traded at P/E NTM of ~12x. As valuation drifted toward ~15x in mid-2015, the stock was baking in higher expectations, and perhaps as a result didn't provide sufficient margin of safety. In hindsight, that was also a good time to sell the stock. It is always hard if not impossible to predict where a valuation peak might occur, but knowing that valuations are elevated usually provides a strong-enough signal for the value investor to trim position or exit the stock. As of this writing the stock was trading around P/E NTM of ~10x, once again offering a potentially attractive valuation level for a value investor to consider buying the stock.

AAPL P/E NTM

When analyzing valuation, it is often helpful to review investing blogs and popular media to get a sense of overall sentiment surrounding a stock, after taking into account recent quarterly earnings results. If you find that noticeably elevated valuation is occuring concurrently with general euphoria about the stock following strong recent quarterly results, then you know you are probably on the right path concluding diminished margin of safety at prevailing levels of stock price.

I have used other more exotic methods of interpreting what's baked into the stock price, using methods like residual income modeling, or incorporating option pricing data into highly complex quantitative models. I have had mixed results with those approaches, and prefer to use the simpler visual approach I have described here. Simplicity is almost always preferable over complexity when it comes to investing. If you never fully understood how a tool worked before using it, you are probably not going to like the outcome from investing based on that tool.

Bullish, Bearish or Neutral?

Its time to decide what to do with the stock – Buy, Sell or do nothing. As you can imagine, this decision making process brings together all the analysis you have done on the stock. In the frameworks below I have used EPS estimates as the decision vector to represent fundamentals, but this could also be done with other metrics like revenues or FCF instead. In each of the charts below you are comparing your Base Case scenario with the sellside consensus, and what's baked into the stock price (buyside consensus), to determine whether there is room for value arbitrage. The two most important elements in this comparison are your own estimates, and those you estimate to represent the buyside consensus. Sellside consensus estimates are of secondary importance in this process.

The next chart illustrates the most bullish scenario, in which your estimates are significantly higher than those baked into the stock. Sellside estimates may be somewhere in between, or closer to buyside consensus.

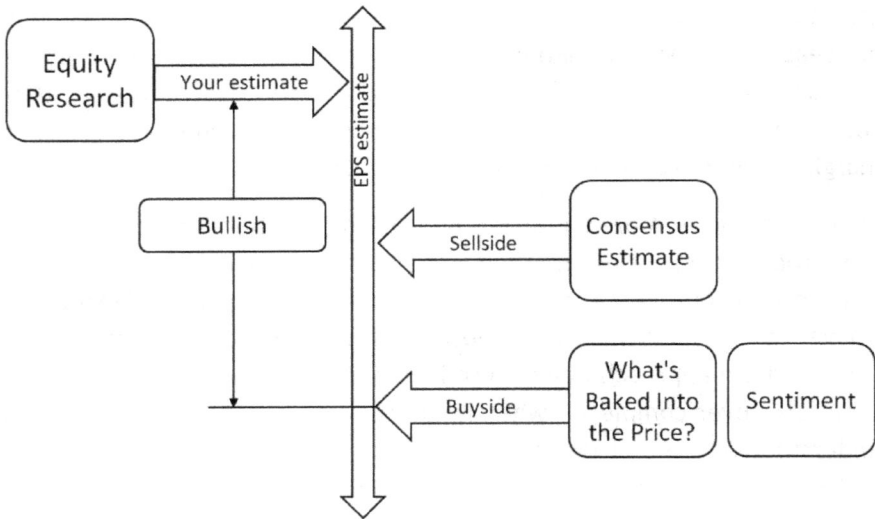

This scenario suggests that if actual company fundamentals were to perform closer to your estimates, then the buyside would be positively surprised, and the stock price would appreciate, allowing you to monetize your investment. Sellside estimates would follow company fundamentals and also appreciate in tandem, supporting higher stock prices.

The next two charts show two derivative scenarios. In the scenario in the next chart, your estimates are similar to those already baked into the stock price. This is a neutral scenario, because if the company performs in line with your estimates, that would not be a big positive surprise to other investors, and the stock would not necessarily appreciate even if results were strong. Sellside estimates are lower, and they would drift up to follow company fundamentals, again without necessarily driving the stock price higher. This was in fact my assessment of the situation when I maintained a Hold rating on AAPL stock from late-2014 through 2015. As it turned out, the company's performance was significantly better than both my estimates and those baked into the stock price. This led to AAPL stock price appreciating initially from late-2014 through mid-2015, as it should have done. Invariably the problem with such stock price appreciation is that it drives up both buyside and sellside expectations for future results, making it harder for the company to deliver upside surprises.

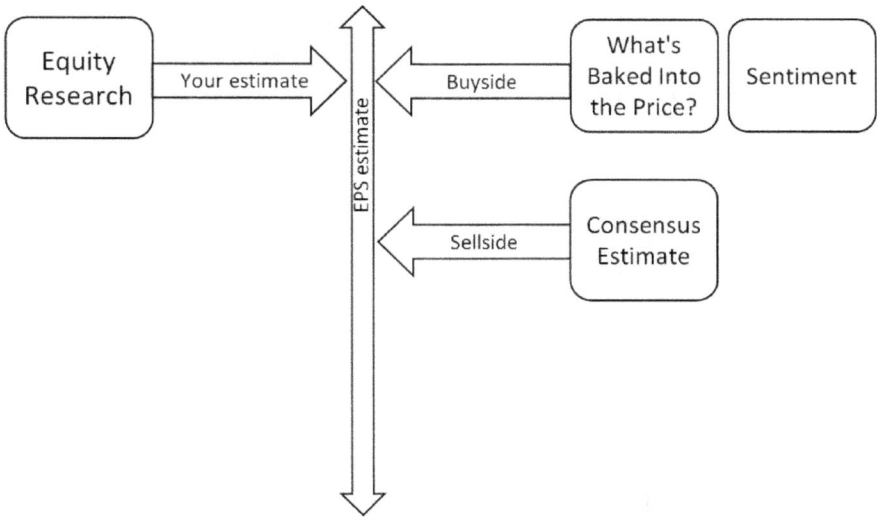

In the chart below, I show a scenario with sellside consensus estimates near buyside consensus, both of which are below your estimates. This would be a bullish scenario, as discussed earlier.

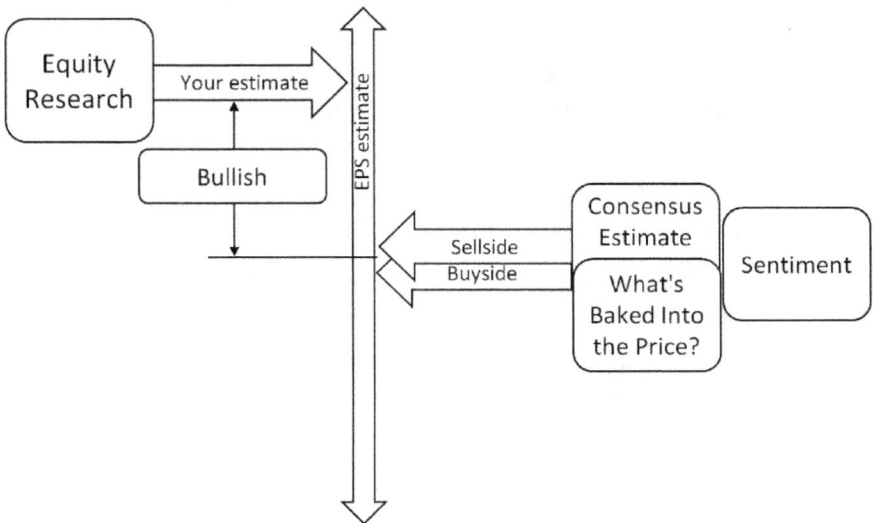

The chart below illustrates the opposite, or a bearish scenario in which your estimates are significantly below the buyside estimates baked into the stock price. Again it wouldn't matter too much whether sellside estimates were in between, or closer to buyside estimates.

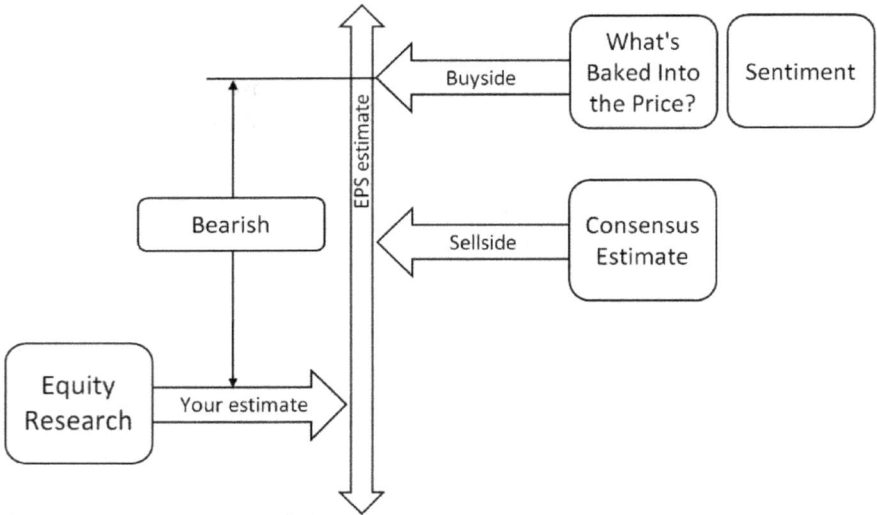

If you are right and company fundamentals perform near your expectations, that would serve as a large disappointment for other investors and the stock price would decrease meaningfully. Sellside estimates again would follow company fundamentals. Similar to what we discussed under the bullish scenario, recurring disappointments would have the effect of decimating buyside and sellside estimates, lowering the bar for the company to beat expectations when business turns again.

The next two chart show two derivative scenarios. In the scenario in the next chart, your estimates are similar to those already baked into the stock price. This is a neutral scenario, because if the company performs in line with your estimates, that would not be a big negative surprise to other investors, and the stock would not necessarily decline even if results were weak.

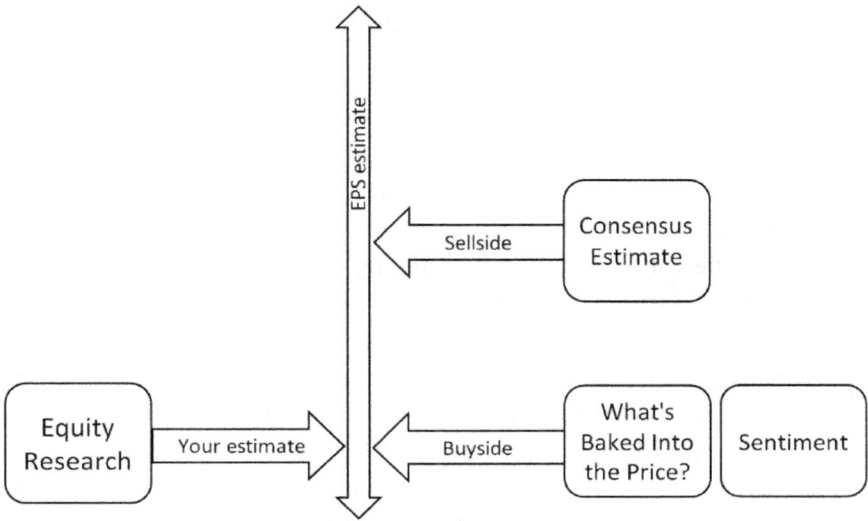

In the the chart below, I show a scenario with sellside consensus estimates near buyside consensus, both of which are above your estimates. This would be a bearish scenario, as discussed earlier.

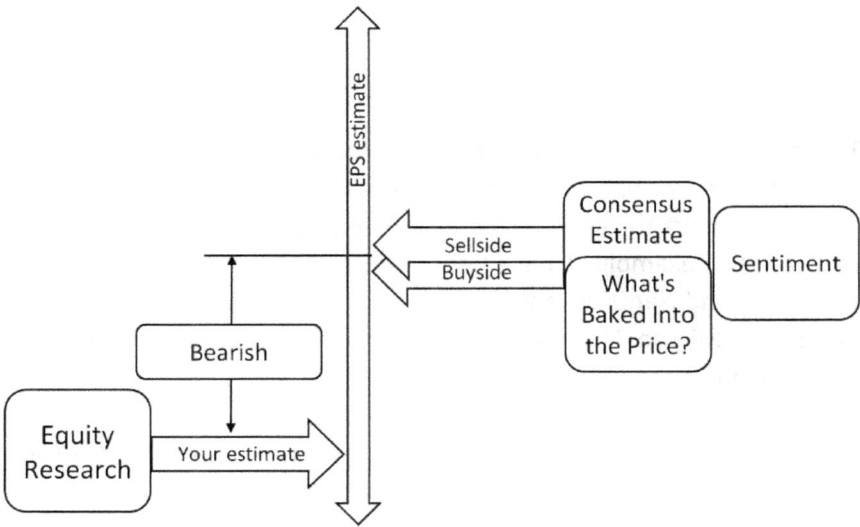

Discounted Cash Flow Analysis – Garbage In Garbage Out

Discounted Cash Flow analysis, or DCF as it is called, is the definitive technique of valuing an investment, when expected future cash flows and the risk profile of the investment are known with reasonable certainty. That is usually never the case with any stock, much less a technology stock. The trouble starts with picking a value for the risk-free rate, and that's supposed to be the easiest part. Estimating all the remaining parameters gets to be progressively more difficult, not to mention the whole process requires implicit subscription to the Capital Asset Pricing Model (CAPM), which drives the cost of capital calculation. After struggling for a long time and finally generating a large number of low-confidence estimates to plug into the DCF, it is likely to spit out a valuation such that >50% of the calculated value is driven by the terminal value of the firm. A ridiculously unproductive outcome of a huge amount of work. I have basically never used DCF as a valuation basis to come up with any stock recommendation, and I must say I never missed it.

While the DCF approach isn't my favorite one for valuation of tech stocks, it is still an indispensable technique for other types of analyses, such as Return On Invested Capital (ROIC) analysis. I have included an example of ROIC analysis later in this chapter.

Other Valuation Techniques

The chart below captures various other techniques that I have used at different times for valuation. I tend to do valuation using multiples most often, and resort to other techniques only as needed depending on the situation. For example, I have used sum of parts for valuing Samsung Electronics and SanDisk, and have done replacement cost analysis for SanDisk and Micron. I have moved away from using residual income based valuation, and have virtually never used DCF or liquidation value analysis as standalone or supplemental measures of intrinsic value. I wouldn't be surprised if there were other exotic valuation methods that I am not even aware of.

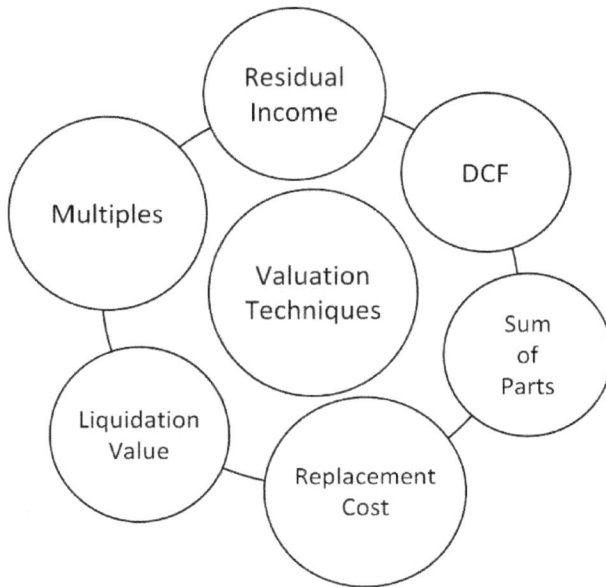

What's Cash Worth?

While the presence of a solid amount of cash and cash equivalents on the balance sheet contributes positively to margin of safety, it is difficult to give too much credit to cash when calculating investment upside. Said differently, cash provides a safety net which could help limit downside risk, but not necessarily a reason to pay a higher multiple for a stock when trying to estimate investment upside. There are a couple of reasons for this. First, when a company is doing well, management faces greater risk of getting sucked into value-destructive M&A, using cash on the balance sheet. Second, if and when growth slows, or well before that happens, investors will start clamoring for cash returns in the form of share repurchases or dividends. If majority of the cash is located overseas, as is often the case with tech companies, then only a small portion of all the cash is immediately available for shareholder returns.

If a good chunk of the cash is located domestically, and management has provided clear guidance about how shareholder returns will be executed, then such use of cash can be explicitly built into forecasts, and will be reflected in lower sharecount or dividend payments or both – again obviating the need to separately give credit to cash on the balance sheet. If the company is doing well and its shares are reasonably well valued, then repurchasing those shares at prevailing (healthy) levels may not necessarily represent best use of cash.

Replacement Cost Analysis Case Study

The chart below shows a sample analysis of Micron's fab replacement cost. The analysis starts with estimates of Micron's fab capacity for DRAM and NAND – two different types of memory products.

DRAM node	Wafer Capacity (KWSPM)	Cost per 10K WSPM ($, m)	Replacement Cost ($, m)
30nm	150	400	6,000
25nm	120	525	6,300
20nm	35	700	2,450
Micron Total	305		14,750
Less Inotera	100	400	4,000
Net Micron DRAM	205		**10,750**
NAND node	Wafer Capacity (KWSPM)	Cost per 10K WSPM ($, m)	Replacement Cost ($, m)
20nm	100	375	3,750
16nm	150	475	7,125
3D	5	700	350
Micron Total	255		11,225
Less Intel	50	350	1,750
Net Micron NAND	205		**9,475**
Total Micron Fabs			20,225

Semiconductor manufacturing capacity is measured in terms of wafer starts per month (WSPM). This is followed by estimates of cost of different types of capacity. Assuming all the assumptions are reasonable, this framework suggests the replacement cost of Micron's total memory manufacturing capacity was around $20B as of this writing, at which time,

Micron stock carried a market capitalization of ~$11B, a nearly 50% discount to the replacement cost of its factories.

Momentum Indicators and Catalysts

Momentum indicators and catalysts can help inform near term business dynamics, as well as potential reactions expected from other investors. The chart below captures different types of catalysts for technology stocks.

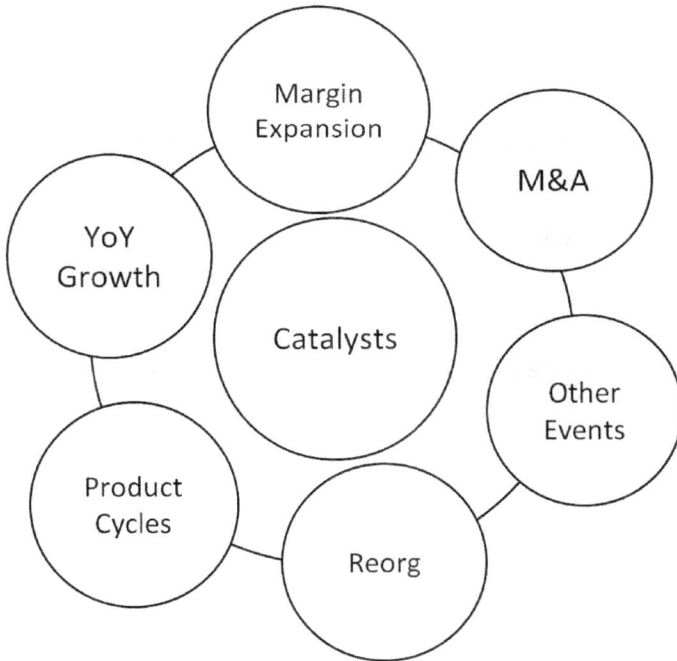

This type of information can be used to guide trading in a particular stock for which an investment decision has already been made. Identifying and understanding such catalysts is helpful even if the exact timing or direction of a particular catalyst cannot be definitively determined in advance. For example, a stock trading down after a negative catalyst might offer an attractive entry point to buy, or conversely a stock trading up after a positive catalyst might provide a good opportunity to take profits.

Events

Trading in technology stocks is influenced by different types of events pertaining to the company or the industry that the stock represents. Such events include company earnings calls, analyst/investor meetings, industry conferences, product launches, executive changes, or M&A announcements. Sometimes such events generate or signal material changes to the company's fundamentals, and deserve closer attention for analysis. However, most often such events do not trigger a meaningful change in fundamentals; yet market participants never miss an opportunity to swing stock prices up or down. This opens windows of opportunities for the patient investor looking to build or wind down her position in the stock.

YoY Revenue Growth

In my experience, the single most important attribute that defines a company's valuation is its projected revenue growth. The chart below captures my estimates of IBM's year-on-year (YoY) revenue growth.

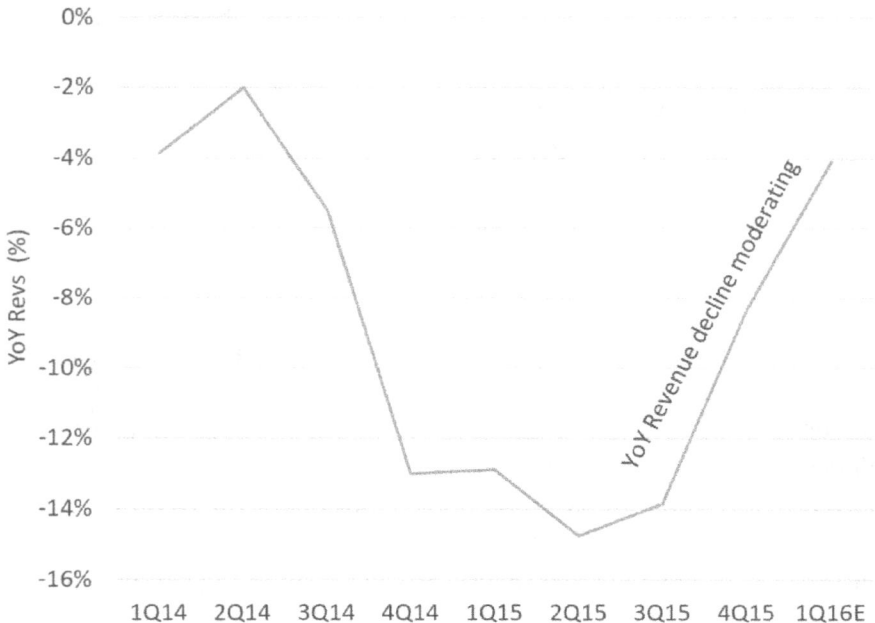

Classifying the company's businesses according to their growth profiles upfront is helpful in narrowing down which pieces are likely to drive value generation (and investor excitement) due to their growth potential. Later on this would also come in handy to do a sum of parts valuation analysis.

An inflection is a meaningful change in the direction of the YoY line shown in the chart above. I have noticed that inflections in YoY revenues (or earnings, cash flow etc.) tend to drive meaningful changes in stock prices for technology stocks. This is primarily because a class of investors referred to as "momentum investors" focus on identifying such inflections in advance, to profit from them on a shorter-term basis.

Margin Expansion

Investors tend to like stocks for which the underlying business is generating increasing levels of profitability. This could be a transient or structural/secular dynamic. One metric of profitability is gross margins. The next chart shows my estimates for IBM's gross margins on an annual basis.

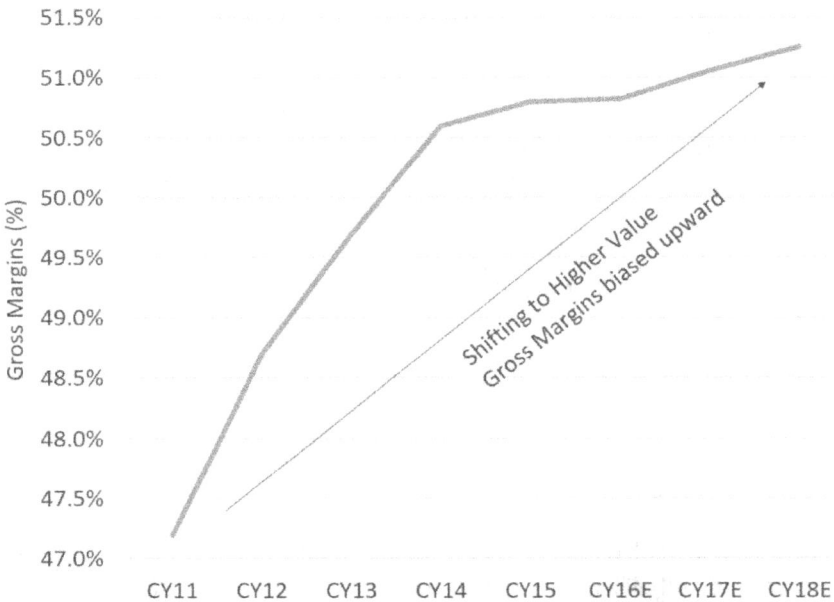

As you can see, strategic and structural changes executed by management seem to be having the effect of raising IBM's gross margins. While margin expansion can be trumped by revenue declines in the short term, it can amplify the effect of revenue stabilization or growth later on, by driving faster growth in earnings or cash flow – a dynamic that is commonly referred to as "operating leverage".

Buy/Sell Discipline

The chart illustrates a rather basic construct, which suggests that when the target price for a stock has been reached, that it should be sold or bought, as the case may be.

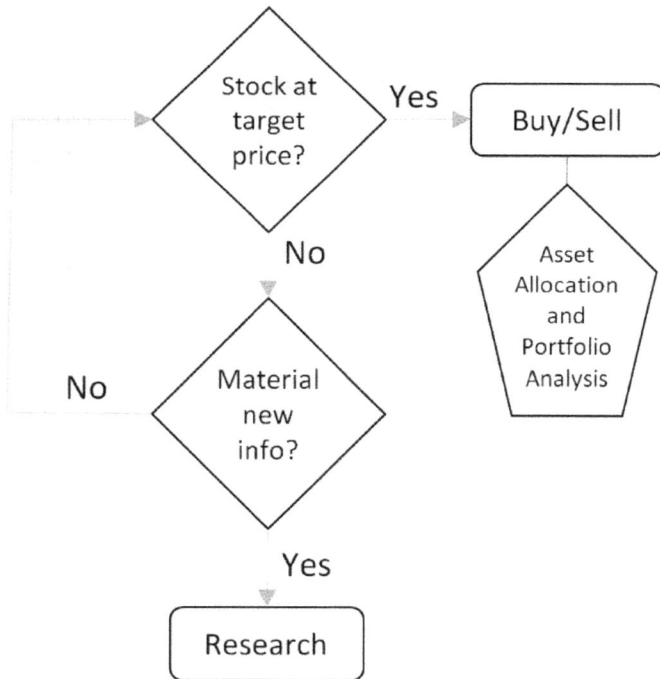

In reality however, I have noticed that in rising markets, investors often "forget" their sell discipline, often with the hope that there might be additional upside as other investors gravitate towards a winning idea.

Conversely, in a bear market, investors keep selling or shorting stocks, often below the net-cash or liquidation values of underlying assets, assuming that other investors will continue to discard those stocks. This dynamic is actually an investment strategy pursued by a sizeable number of investment managers, and it is called "momentum investing".

Putting it all together

In the last two chapters we discussed processes for company analysis and valuation analysis. It is time to put the individual pieces together to form a better understanding of investment risk, and how risk can mitigated through value investing. The next chapter applies the concept of Margin of Safety, a central concept in value investing, to technology stocks.

Brace yourself, as you are about to enter uncharted waters, that traditional value investors have preferred to stay out of.

Chapter 6 – MARGIN of SAFETY IN TECHNOLOGY INVESTMENTS

I learnt the concept of "Margin of Safety" in Benjamin Graham's famous book "Intelligent Investor", and have since become both a student and a preacher of value investing. Interestingly enough, some of the most respected value investors tend to avoid tech stocks, explicitly because they think tech stocks are too hard to analyze – and they would be correct, of course. This is what really gave me the idea for applying principles of value investing to tech, and more recently for writing this book.

Margin of safety is indicative of protection from permanent loss of investment capital. The chart below illustrates the concept of margin of safety. The fundamental driver of margin of safety in a stock investment, is the purchase price paid for the stock.

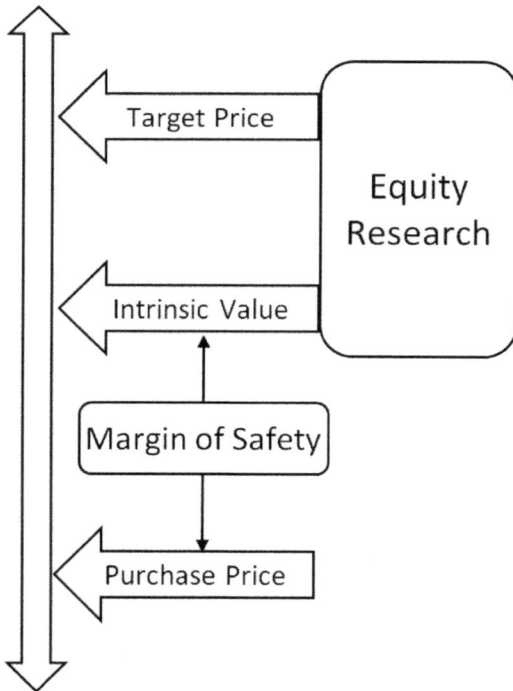

So the entire equity research effort then is focused on analyzing a business and coming up with a conservative estimate of intrinsic value, such that you can then patiently wait to buy the stock at a significant discount to that estimate of intrinsic value. Once a purchase has been made, you can then hold the stock until your underlying investment thesis is realized, without being overly concerned about interim gyrations and volatility of the market.

To fully understand the importance of margin of safety, it is necessary to first re-examine the definition of risk. For a value investor, risk is the probability of permanent loss of capital. In other words, risk is different from volatility, which is more a statistical measure (variance) of short-term changes in market prices of stocks. Notably value investors have a different definition of risk than the one that is taught in top-school MBA programs, and the one that is used in mathematical calculations as a measure of risk. The academic concept of risk stems from Nobel Prize winning work, which is commonly referred to as Modern Portfolio Theory (MPT), and Capital Asset Pricing Model (CAPM). The mathematical elegance and convenience of MPT and CAPM have trumped their perverse effect on investor behavior when used as the primary frameworks for thinking about risk. The perverse effect is that followers of MPT and CAPM believe that higher investment returns cannot be had without underwriting higher investment risk, for which volatility is the chosen proxy.

Value investing is contrarian by definition, and seeks to identify investments that can generate superior returns, while undertaking minimal risk – so the exact opposite of what MPT and CAPM postulate.

Drivers of Margin of Safety

The chart below illustrates my view of the four factors that drive margin of safety for an investment in a technology stock. There are at least two if not three additional factors here in my framework compared to the original process laid out by Benjamin Graham. Some people today refer to Graham's original value investing process as "deep value investing", perhaps because his basis of investing was primarily a severe valuation discount, which in most cases involved stocks trading below liquidation values of underlying company assets. His process may or may not have involved a recent stock price decline leading to severe undervaluation.

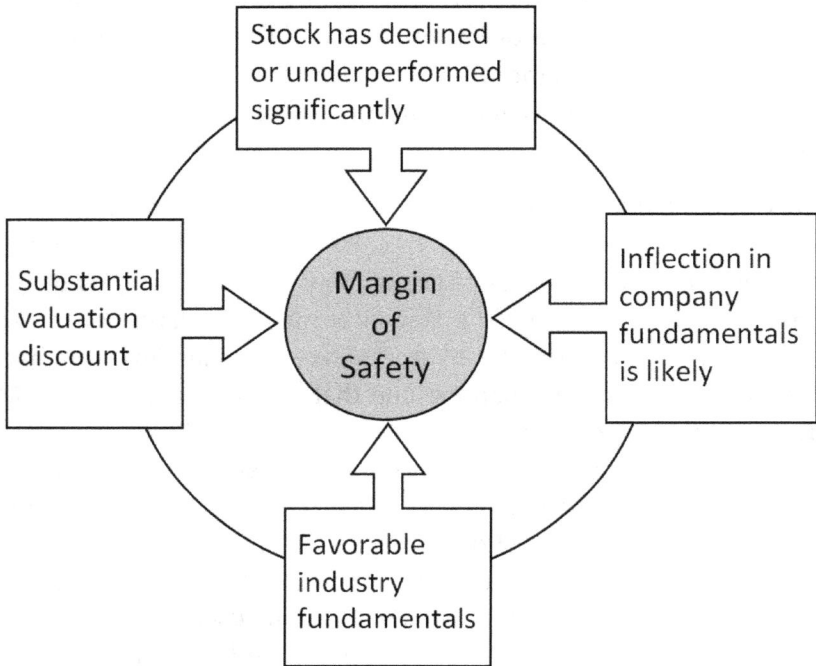

Stock has declined or underperformed significantly

Substantial valuation discount

Margin of Safety

Inflection in company fundamentals is likely

Favorable industry fundamentals

Substantial Valuation Discount

While Graham was very successful applying his framework of estimating intrinsic value, as described in his legendary book "Security Analysis", his approach was based primarily on liquidation value of assets. Since technology companies today derive much of their value from assets that may not be easily liquefiable (e.g. intangible assets, intellectual property, brand value, specialized assets), Graham's original approach does not transfer over easily to investing in technology stocks. As we discussed in the previous chapter on valuation, the goal of equity research is to come up with estimates for intrinsic value under different business conditions, based on thorough analysis of company and industry fundamentals. Accordingly, the valuation discount referenced in the chart above is a comparison between the prevailing stock price in the market, and your own independent estimates for intrinsic value. If a given stock is trading at a price that represents a ~50% or more discount to your estimates of intrinsic value, then it is potentially a worthy candidate to consider as an investment.

Stock has declined or underperformed significantly

Today's equity markets abound in short-term profit seekers who do little if anything in the form of equity research, especially when it comes to technology stocks. Still, even if purely by chance, it is possible that a substantial majority of market participants at a given time are holding a stock because they are correctly bullish about its prospects, even though they may be unaware of the reasons. This will often manifest itself in the form of recent stock appreciation or outperformance (relative to a relevant index like the S&P 500 for example) – a situation that you as a value investor must be cautious of, because such consensus bullishness must have invariably translated into higher expectations that the company might find difficult to meet or beat.

Checking for such recent stock appreciation may also be a quick screen that could be used to deprioritize equity research on stocks that do not deserve immediate focus. Conversely, you will probably be well served to shift your focus toward stocks that have declined in value over recent periods, especially if you also have additional industry-specific insight about an investor misunderstanding of fundamentals. In fact, some "value-style" mutual funds use recent stock underperformance as a primary criteria for selecting their investments, with or without additional equity research.

Inflection in Company Fundamentals is Likely

This factor is uniquely new in my framework compared to Graham's original process. It also gets to the core premise of this book – that *if you have industry expertise in Technology, then you are in a better position compared to the average investor, to determine if a positive inflection in a given tech company's fundamentals is likely*. Forming a deep understanding of a company's products, technologies, and interactions with the markets it participates in, should enable an investment thesis based on anticipated inflections in company fundamentals. The chart below illustrates various elements involved in determining if such an inflection in company fundamentals is likely.

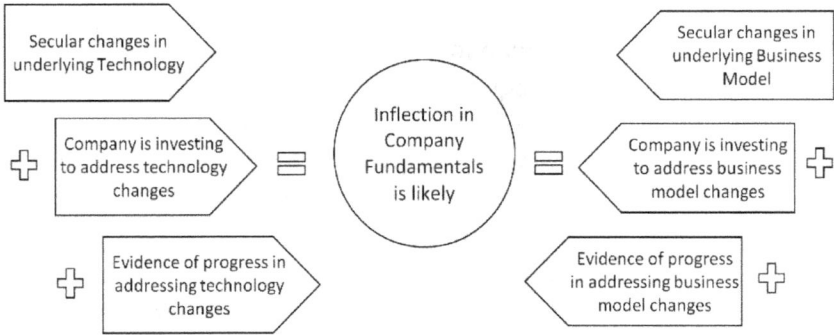

At the root of a prospective inflection in business fundamentals lies a secular change in underlying products or technologies. One example of such a change would be the shift occurring in the wireless base station market over the last few years. Wireless base stations used to cost ~$45K each five years ago. Today, they cost ~$10-20K, and costs are expected to decline further. When a complex system like a base station goes through such cost structure disruption, it drives design changes which affect selection of individual components. More expensive components like high-end FPGAs (field-programmable gate array) in this case were replaced by a combination of DSP (digital signal processor) and ASSP (application specific standard processor). This created opportunities for Cavium (NASDAQ: CAVM), while truncating the market for Altera (now part of Intel) and Xilinx (NASDAQ: XLNX).

Of course the mere presence of such potential is not sufficient, and it must be evident that the company has a similar view of the market as you, and is actively investing to capitalize on the changes.

Finally, you must feel convinced that the company's investments to capitalize on changing market dynamics are translating into real progress, and meaningful upward revisions to business fundamentals are likely. Notice I said "feel" and not "know". It is rare if at all possible to know with any level of certainty that a particular company's business is about to improve meaningfully. The best you can hope to accomplish realistically is a compelling belief that the company is on the right path, customer and vendor feedback is supportive, and overall industry analysis reinforces the general idea of improvement in company fundamentals.

Favorable industry fundamentals

This is another factor that is uniquely new in my framework compared to Graham's. A number of factors contribute toward favorable industry fundamentals, as shown in the chart below.

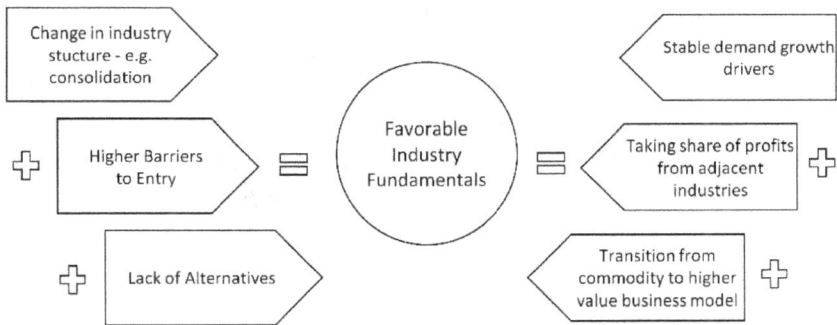

Industry composition, and potential for (or positive impact from) consolidation is probably the easiest to analyze quantitatively. One framework I have found useful for such analysis is the Herfindahl-Hirschman Index (HHI), which measures industry concentration. The higher the industry concentration, the higher the potential for the industry to be healthy, in terms of both stability of the profit pool and distribution of profits among individual participants. Inflections in HHI tend to be catalysts for changes in industry dynamics.

Higher barriers to entry and a lack of alternatives or substitutes further solidify the stability of the industry profit pool by making it difficult for new players to enter the market. As long as the industry is not catering to a potentially diminishing market opportunity (like Hard Disk Drives for example), it's not as critical to know the exact growth rate of the end market. Ability to take share from (aka disrupt) adjacent markets can

111

amplify near-term growth rates. For example, the NAND Flash industry is taking share from Hard Disk Drives (HDD), and this will continue to have the effect of powering higher growth rates for NAND, while depressing growth rates for HDD. Ability to leap from selling a commodity product to selling higher-value systems can also structurally change industry dynamics for the better. Going back to the NAND example, as the NAND industry increasingly caters to high-end professional storage applications, as opposed to "commodity" consumer storage applications, it has a chance to grow the industry profit pool over time.

Needless to say studying company and industry dynamics to form an a priori view on a stock investment is difficult even for a technology industry expert, and practically impossible for a tech-industry outsider, such as a pure finance professional. *This means the average investor by definition invests without the benefit of a high level of margin of safety in technology stocks. This is also why renowned value investors tend to stay away from technology stocks – because they are brave enough to admit their limited abilities in this space.*

Industry Knowledge Does Not Come Easy

Studying technology and business dynamics in the industry is not something you can do without leaving your office and getting out in the field. This is an area where having prior training in engineering or the sciences can dramatically improve your chances of forming a high-confidence understanding of prevailing trends. There's nothing you can read or watch or crunch numbers on from within your office on your computer to bypass the process of forming trusted relationships with industry experts, carefully assimilating bits and pieces of information over time, and using your knowledgebase of technology and products to interpret a picture of prevailing industry dynamics. This is also the part that I have seen generalist investors (including value investors) struggle with. Here's a quick analogy – if you aren't a doctor, then you cannot be relied upon for accurately diagnosing what's wrong with a patient, no matter how much you research about the symptoms on the internet – there's simply no substitute for a trained doctor, except perhaps in the most trivial cases of bruises or bumps or other ailments like that. Likewise, identifying exactly what changes might be transpiring at the deepest levels of high-tech products and underlying technologies is not something anyone can expect a generalist investor to be able to accomplish with high confidence. The only way to cheat the system here would be for the generalist investor to have a trusted advisor that she can count on for explaining what she needs to know, all the time. Still, this is bound to be an imperfect process with plenty of room for details to be lost in translation, and the investor may not be able to build as much conviction as she would like to with her investments.

Importance of Judgment

Intuition and judgment are irreplaceably important in every aspect of life, and investing is no different. A solid fundamental understanding of the technology industry combined with diligent analysis of individual technologies and companies should over time instill and harden a sense of deep-rooted judgment. Confidence and comfort in your own judgment as an analyst ultimately forms the root of trust in the chain of activities that build conviction in an investment. Obviously judgment doesn't come overnight, and nor does conviction. This is what makes the assessment of margin of safety difficult, particularly for technology stocks, for which investors are often missing one or more ingredient elements of the conviction building process.

Let's look at a couple of case studies to better understand how margin of safety works.

Case Study # 1: Micron

Covering Micron (NASDAQ: MU) has been fascinating, and a huge learning experience for me. I think it is almost a perfect example to demonstrate many aspects of the discussion in this chapter. I recommended Micron as a stock to Buy in 2012, based on positive assessments on all four of the factors that I believe drive margin of safety.

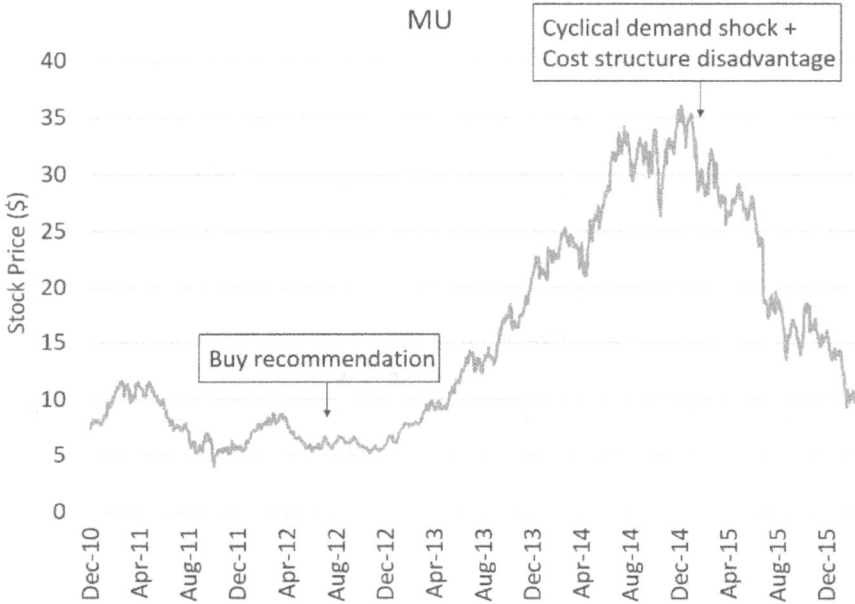

Stock had declined meaningfully and had underperformed the S&P 500. Micron had underperformed in the period leading up to 2012, so it wasn't exactly a darling stock - a great place to dig in as a value-oriented tech investor.

Trading at discount valuation. Micron was trading at a Price to Book (P/B) of ~1x, which in tech usually means that the company is viewed as a low quality investment.

Industry fundamentals were favorable. My analysis of technology and industry fundamentals suggested that: 1) secular technology challenges in semiconductor cost scaling would structurally change the competitive

114

dynamics in DRAM and NAND - Micron's main products, and 2) industry consolidation would improve competitive dynamics in DRAM.

Company fundamentals were likely to inflect positively. Micron had historically been a technology laggard, with its DRAM and NAND product cost structures lagging significantly behind industry leader Samsung's. As fundamental technology limitations constrained Samsung's ability to improve its cost structure, I believed that Micron would have a better chance of catching up.

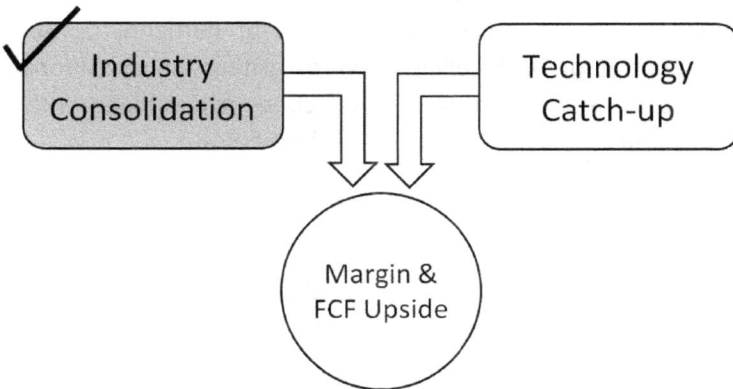

When I first introduced my "industry change" thesis, it was immediately dismissed by investors as an overly optimistic scenario that was unlikely to play out. However over the next 18 months or so, industry and company updates were miraculously consistent with my thesis, and drove solid improvement in business fundamentals (i.e. revenues, margins, EPS, cash flow). Accordingly, MU stock appreciated dramatically – five-fold to be specific. While I had seen similar reactions in other stocks previously, the multi-fold appreciation of MU stock was interesting to watch.

I learnt in the process that a stock that nobody would buy at $5.50 because they hadn't done the work and didn't understand the fundamentals, was a stock they would fall over themselves to buy at $11, $20, or even higher. Of course this is the kind of institutional investor behavior that leads to a stock bubble – when a stock that has already appreciated a lot, attracts new supporters and admirers ("bulls"), each of which is eager to justify higher valuations even though they still don't fully understand the fundamentals. MU stock peaked at around $35 in mid-2014.

In mid-to-late-2014, investors started to suspect that some of the cyclical tailwind that Micron's business had enjoyed was about to reverse. From there, the stock started to lose support, as more and more investors gravitated toward the idea of a cyclical shock. Additionally as investors started to look for a reason to sell, they realized that Micron's cost structure was still significantly inferior to Samsung's and this didn't bode well when faced with cyclical degradation of demand. Consequently, investors spent all of 2015 selling down or exiting their positions in MU, largely owing to a shorter-term cyclical concern combined with lack of conviction in industry dynamics. See the chart below.

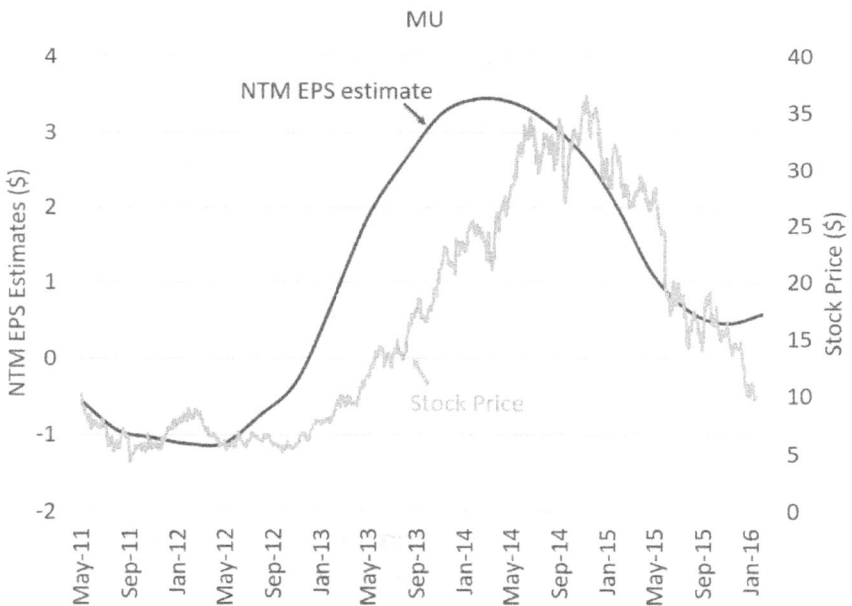

Fast forward to today (early-2016). Micron is trading at ~$10, representing P/B of ~1x, at a roughly 50% discount to the replacement cost of its factories, because investors are worried about macro issues pertaining to China, Europe, and U.S. interest rates. Favorable supply-side industry fundamentals remain virtually unchanged, and additionally, Micron is finally at a point where it can execute on the technology catch-up I mentioned earlier. More than 3 years later, we find once again that investors are still struggling to appreciate fundamentals, and following the herd (again) continuing to sell down the stock.

The Micron case study also makes one more point, which speaks to one of the reasons I am writing this book. Micron was owned by prominent (generalist) value investors over the period noted above, with varying success. As of this writing, some or all of those value investors seem to have largely exited their positions in Micron. It is not clear to me if those who decided to substantially sell down their positions, perhaps at a loss, considered the inflection (owing to cost-structure catch-up) that lies in front of Micron. In other words, within my framework of analysis, it is possible that a number of these value investors (like others) struggled to form a complete understanding of Micron's fundamentals, perhaps due to lack of technology industry expertise – or maybe they got it right, or they succumbed to short-term performance pressure. We will not know for sure until we observe how Micron's fundamentals shape up over the coming months.

What's the downside protection in the Short Run?

Unfortunately often indeterminate. To establish a margin of safety, one has to understand what earnings and cash flow a business is capable of generating over the longer term, and then buy the stock at a compelling price that accounts for unknown errors in analysis. Even if you invest with a solid margin of safety after thorough analysis, that doesn't necessarily mean that the stock will not trade up to 50% or more below your purchase price in the short term, which I would define as a period of ~1 year for tech stocks, but could be longer. The market has a tendency to value companies on next-twelve-month (NTM) earnings estimates, and you will often find strong correlations between the stock price and NTM earnings estimates provided by the sellside – a dynamic that is often questionable, given the buyside has its own analysts who are doing their own independent research.

In situations where market volatility is high, usually due to macro concerns, stocks can get beaten up to a point where the valuation does not make any sense by any measure. But to know this one has to be armed with thorough research in advance, ready to buy stocks that the market is carelessly discarding. Importantly, one has to have confidence in one's research during such times of market-driven duress, which tends to happen every so often. I would venture to say that the mechanism that drives market duress is fundamentally not that different from what I described above for MU stock. It's a race among short-term investors to "ride" the most popular ideas to make the most money, and exit the positions at just the right time before others fear that the party might be over.

I believe the way to win this race is to do things differently – focus on the longer term, do your own independent research, and be ready to buy stocks when the short-timers are selling as a herd.

Case Study # 2: Apple

Covering Apple was also a tremendous learning experience, charged with emotional debates with investors madly in love with the company and the stock. In late-2014, and through 2015, I recommended that investors be cautious of AAPL stock – in other words, avoid buying AAPL stock. Over that period AAPL traded between $100 and $135. As of the writing of this book, AAPL stock was trading at <$95. How low or high the stock trades from these levels is irrelevant – the point is that investors were disappointed with Apple, in spite of the company delivering record results. Fundamental disappointment was compounded by broader macro weakness over concerns around China, among other things, with China being among the most important markets for Apple.

AAPL

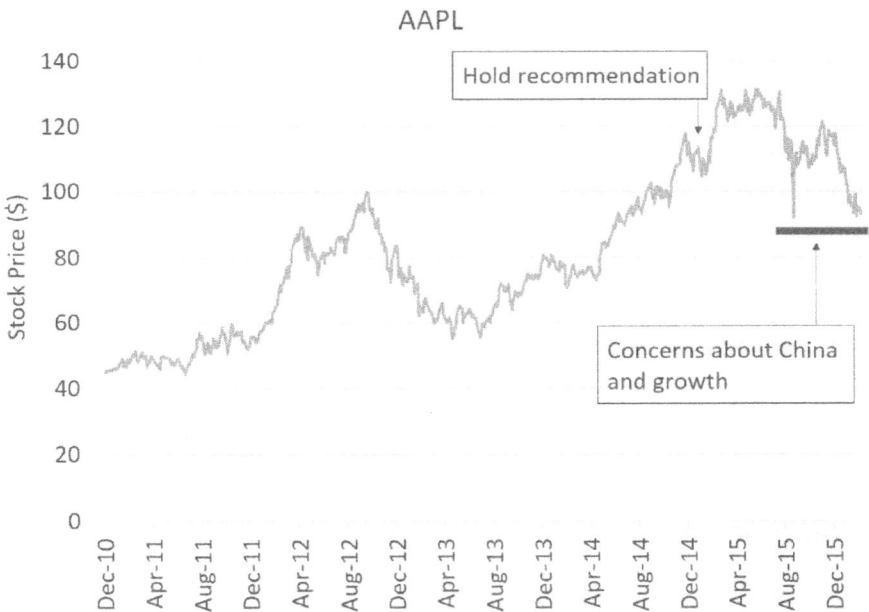

The stock materially appreciated and outperformed from late-2013 to mid-2015. Clearly it was not a stock that was being discarded by the market, even though bulls on the stock would argue that it was trading at a discount to other tech stocks like GOOG or FB. This is a yellow flag for a value investor, as it suggests that investor expectations might be too high and there is elevated risk of disappointment.

AAPL's forward P/E (aka P/E NTM) had increased from historical avg. of ~13x to ~15x. Changes in a stock's valuation multiple can signal changes in investor expectations. If a stock is trading at a higher P/E multiple, by definition investors are expecting the company to report better earnings than those reflected in sellside consensus estimates, off which forward P/E is measured.

Industry fundamentals unfavorable with rising competition. Around the time I first started covering Samsung Electronics a few years ago, I switched from using iPhone/iPad to using a Samsung phone/tablet running Android, while my wife continued to use iPhone/iPad. I knew that this would put me on level footing and a position of advantage compared to the average AAPL bull, who was only familiar with Apple products but not as familiar with the competition – I know I wasn't until I switched. I must say that I was completely blown away by the capabilities of Samsung's hardware, and the Android OS, so much so that I converted my entire productivity and entertainment process flows from iOS to Android. I still admired the iPhones and iPads at home, but with very clear knowledge of their deficiencies. When you combine Google's highly capable Cloud Services with a range of hardware makers for Android-based phones and tablets, you get a highly disruptive force which is also most relevant to the fastest growing portion of the market – emerging markets. As of late-2014, Apple was already capturing the majority of profits in the Smartphone hardware market, and there wasn't really too much more profit share for Apple to take. Clearly this was not fantastic in terms of an industry setup for AAPL stock.

Sustainability of company-fundamentals would be questioned. My analysis of Google's Cloud Services business suggested that Google was monetizing a much larger installed base of (lower-cost) Android devices, while Apple was limiting itself to a smaller (more-expensive) iOS device installed base, growth in which would be increasingly driven by China, where consumers aren't as accustomed to paying for premium content, like they are in the developed world. To cement its longer-term growth prospects against a backdrop of slowing iPhone hardware growth, I believed that Apple would need to find a way to develop and refine its Cloud Services, in which it was behind Google, and then find a way to monetize those services across a larger installed base – i.e. beyond just iOS devices. When I first introduced this thesis in 2014, a number of investors found it interesting, but I recall a couple of tech-specialists at large hedge funds telling me that I didn't have a good understanding of Apple's business model. As of the writing of this book in early-2016, Apple Music was being rolled out to Android devices – a first for Apple to introduce its Cloud Service to non-iOS users, while AAPL stock had taken a beating.

What happens to AAPL from here? With its stock price in the $90s, AAPL could be said to be approaching value territory (see chart below) -

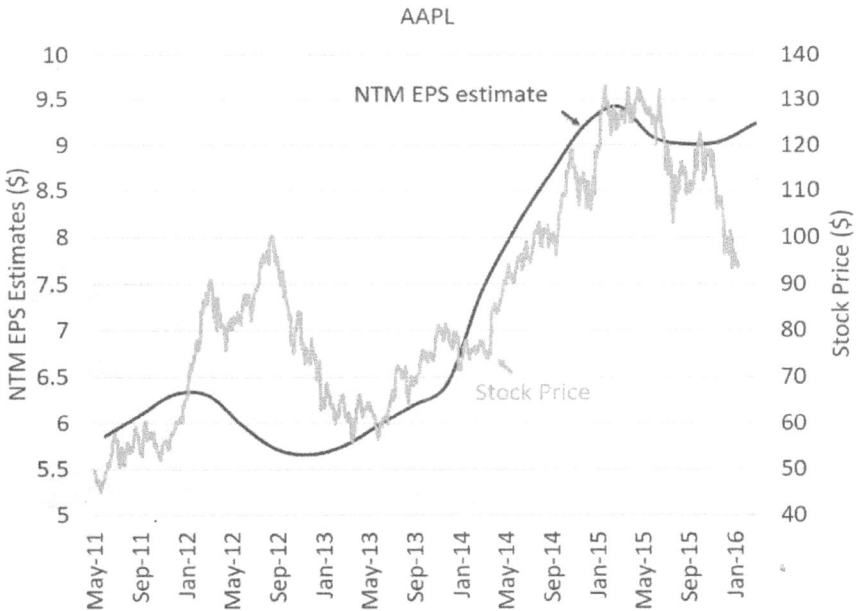

AAPL

The lower the stock goes, and the more the NTM EPS estimates get cut on the sellside, the higher the margin of safety would be. You want growth investors with their fanatic imagination out of the stock, so that value investors can buy it for the solid investment it represents, for the next few years. A large and growing installed base of iPhone and iPad provide an "annuity" cushion, as these users come back to upgrade their devices every 2 years or so for iPhone, and 4+ years for iPad. Apple has enjoyed strong brand power, particularly in emerging markets, where it is most relevant. In addition to Apple's strategic progress with Cloud Services, management also seems to be consciously making older products (e.g. iPhone 5s) available for longer in growth markets like India. Apple's strong cash holdings combined with conservative accounting anticipating large repatriations of cash provide good valuation support through the prospect of stock buybacks and dividend growth.

The next chart below shows that even if you assume a 5-to-10% shipment decline for iPhone in 2016, iPhone (and iOS) installed base would remain roughly stable.

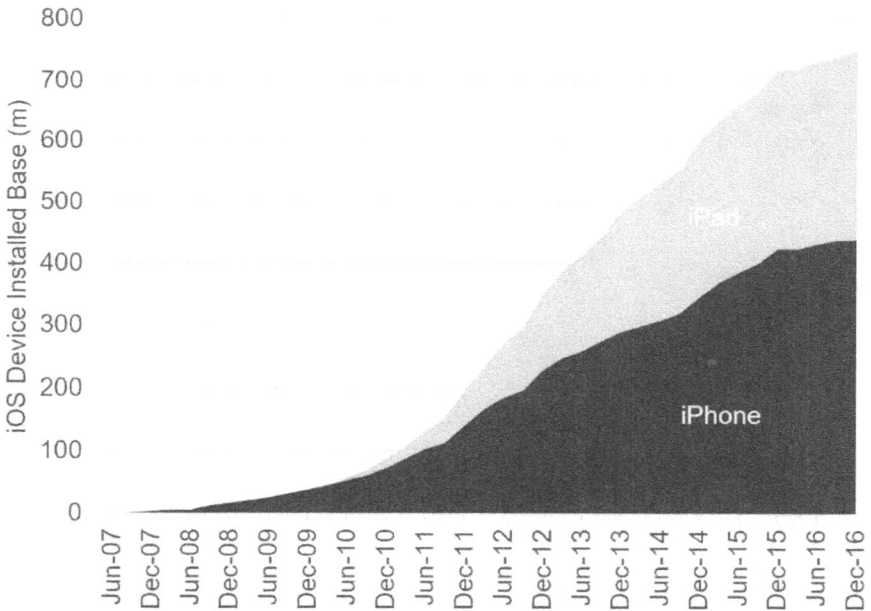

This provides a big opportunity for Apple to better monetize its existing and new services across such users, as well as eventually extend those services to Android users. Within my process, data in these two charts provide a margin of safety in AAPL as an investment, a phenomenon that may not be as well understood by the market.

Case Study # 3: NVDA – How Shorting Works in Value Investing

Given the general directional bias of the market is upward, taking a short position in a stock deserves more caution compared to long positions, and must be driven by a combination of structural or secular dynamics, and definitive catalysts. Shorting stocks just because valuation may have wandered off and become too rich in the short term, would probably not offer sufficient margin of safety. The chart below illustrates a case study with NVDA in 2010.

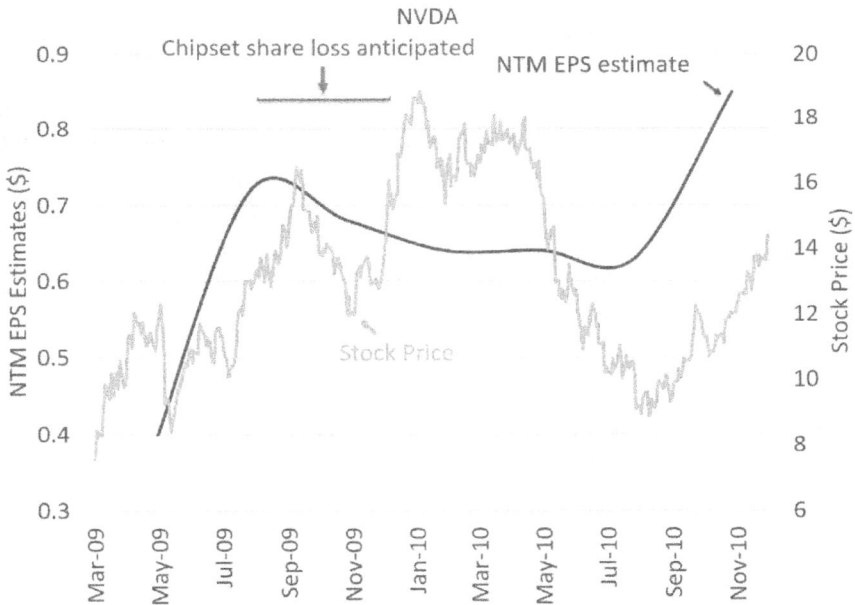

My industry analysis and interpretation of Intel's product roadmap in 2009 had consistently pointed to high risk of impending PC chipset share loss for Nvidia, due to competitor Intel's shift toward an integrated CPU+chipset strategy, something that non-tech-savvy investors would have struggled to identify on their own. The market was predictably oblivious to this dynamic, and NVDA stock spent the latter part of 2009 appreciating significantly. If you consider the margin of safety framework introduced in this chapter, remembering to flip the direction of the factors for a short thesis vs. long thesis, you will see that a combination of recent stock outperformance, higher valuation, and unfavorable industry dynamics had created a strong case for shorting the stock around high-$teens. Over the next nine months, the stock declined more than 50%, generating strong returns from a low-risk short investment. The catalyst in this case, as is most often the case, was degradation of earnings.

This is one example where the timing of specific underlying fundamentals turned this into a short-duration investment, rather than a 2-to-5 year investment. This example also underscores another tenet of value investing – to exit your position (long or short) once your investment thesis has materially played out. To be fair Nvidia unfortunately didn't have much (if any) control over the direction of its chipset business, since its larger competitor/partner Intel decided to shut Nvidia out through integration. Since the chipset mishap, Nvidia has effectively reinvented itself as a company. As of this writing, Nvidia was at the forefront of at least a couple of major technology trends, as we will see in Chapter 8 – Self-driving car, Cloud growth, as well as Virtual Reality.

International Stocks

If you thought investing in domestic (U.S.) tech stocks is hard, wait till you hear about unique issues related to international stocks, in the next chapter.

Chapter 7 – INTERNATIONAL STOCKS: SAMSUNG CASE STUDY

Covering Samsung Electronics (KRX: 005930) was probably the most exciting and challenging learning experience for me, for a number of reasons: as of this writing Samsung Electronics was the largest tech company domiciled outside the U.S., as an engineer I have always been fascinated by the range of technologies that Samsung has achieved a leadership position in, I became the first analyst to cover both Samsung Electronics and Apple concurrently, accessing and interpreting information about Samsung was difficult and required frequent visits to Korea, and I was able to form a non-consensus view of Samsung's memory and foundry businesses – this helped me build relationships with a number of fund managers based in Asia, a privilege that differentiated me from my U.S. based peers. The chart below captures some of the challenges you might face when analyzing international stocks.

Accounting

I built a model for Samsung from scratch, using audited financial statements posted on Samsung's investor relations (IR) website. Samsung, like other companies in Korea, follows the K-IFRS (Korean – International Financial Reporting Standards) version of accounting standards which as far as I know is virtually identical to global IFRS standards set by the International Accounting Standards Board. I noticed quickly that there was a large dispersion in estimates among the 50+ covering analysts, almost all of which were based in Korea – this included a broad range of estimates for sharecount, which I thought was unusual.

Building a segment (aka "bottom up") model for Samsung was challenging because of the diversity of businesses the company conducted, including Semiconductor (memory and logic chips), Smartphone/Tablet, TV, Display Panel, and Home Appliances. Understanding and modeling key drivers of each of these businesses with a view to anticipating potential inflections, was very time consuming, but well worth the effort. As I did the work, it became clear to me that with its Smartphone business maturing, emphasis would shift back to Semiconductor operations. This became the central theme of my thesis on the stock from 2013-2014.

Embedded within my thesis of DRAM-driven Semiconductor resurgence, which by the way was a contrarian view when I first introduced it, was another curious development in Samsung's foundry business. My work suggested that there was high likelihood that Samsung would snatch leadership of leading-edge 14nm logic chip manufacturing from TSMC, who had been the undisputed incumbent leader for a while. Virtually every investor I spoke with around the world disagreed with me. Knowing that I had a non-consensus view encouraged me to dedicate even more resources to analyzing the topic in more detail – an effort that proved to be quite rewarding in the end, as Samsung took market share away from TSMC.

Language and Culture

Even though Korea has been home to a large number of Americans for some time, and a growing number of Korean businesses are becoming multi-national, business in Korea is still conducted predominantly in

Korean, within the framework of traditional cultural norms and etiquette. Context is often important and presumed to be well known while communicating. This makes it tricky to interpret conversations even when they are done in English and face to face. Of course interpretation becomes much harder when conversations are done over the phone or via email. It is no wonder then that investors easily and frequently misinterpret communications from Samsung.

Access

Engaging with operations leaders was key to deciphering how the organization moved. I had to routinely flex my Korean language skills to first locate and then direct cab drivers to Samsung's local offices – a fun task that I knew the average investor was probably not up for. Over a period of a couple of years I went from having virtually zero contacts at Samsung to having connections with 50+ managers in different parts of the world across different organizations. The basis for these connections was my genuine desire to learn more about the company, and help investors understand it better – a purpose that almost everyone at the company wanted to help me fulfill.

Not having sufficient access to Samsung's business group leaders, or even investor relations personnel, can be a challenge for investors located outside of Korea.

Corporate Governance, Geopolitical Issues

Samsung is one example of the reality that a great company may not always make a great stock investment in the short-term. Since it dawned on investors in 2013 that the Smartphone market was maturing and competition was increasing, Samsung stock has been in doldrums, trading near P/B of ~1x, and P/E NTM near 10x or lower. I think the stock faces two structural problems, both of which are probably solvable in the long run.

First, given Samsung's relatively high (~20-30%) weighting in the investable Korea country index, portfolio managers find it difficult to be overweight the stock. Domestic funds in Korea have been constrained to hold not more than 10% of their investments in any single stock, though that might be changing. This means that Samsung stock has often been at the mercy of foreign investors, who as we discussed may not always fully understand the company's fundamentals and strategies.

Second, given deceleration in growth, investors shifted their attention to corporate governance issues. Specificially this means investors would be interested in cash returns from Samsung, in the form of dividends or stock buybacks. One approach to potentially address both issues might be to list Samsung stock on a U.S. stock exchange – this has been a topic of interest for many years, though it is not clear whether the company is closer to executing such a multiple listing.

Encouraged by my progress with Samsung, I also built models for SK hynix (Korean memory maker), and TSMC (Taiwan Semiconductor Manufacturing Company), the second largest stock in Asia behind Samsung. Unfortunately I did not have a chance to officially cover either of these two companies.

Technology is globally connected

Analyzing international stocks adds a unique tool to your arsenal, a tool that can contribute substantially to building investment conviction that leads to margin of safety. This can also differentiate you from the average investor who is not as concerned with connecting the dots globally, or deems it too difficult to accomplish.

Building on this idea, the next chapter lays out technology investment themes that span across the industry, globally.

Chapter 8 – TECHNOLOGY INVESTMENT LANDSCAPE

Investing in tech stocks is difficult because the rapid pace of innovation in technology disrupts companies as well as entire industries quickly, and blindly executing to a "buy and hold" strategy in tech can be treacherous for your investments (see the chart below). If you have academic training in engineering, along with industry experience in product development, familiarity with the industry landscape, as well as appetite to continuously learn and update your understanding of the industry, then you stand to be better informed than the average tech investor. Better industry information could then be turned into investment success through the process described in this book.

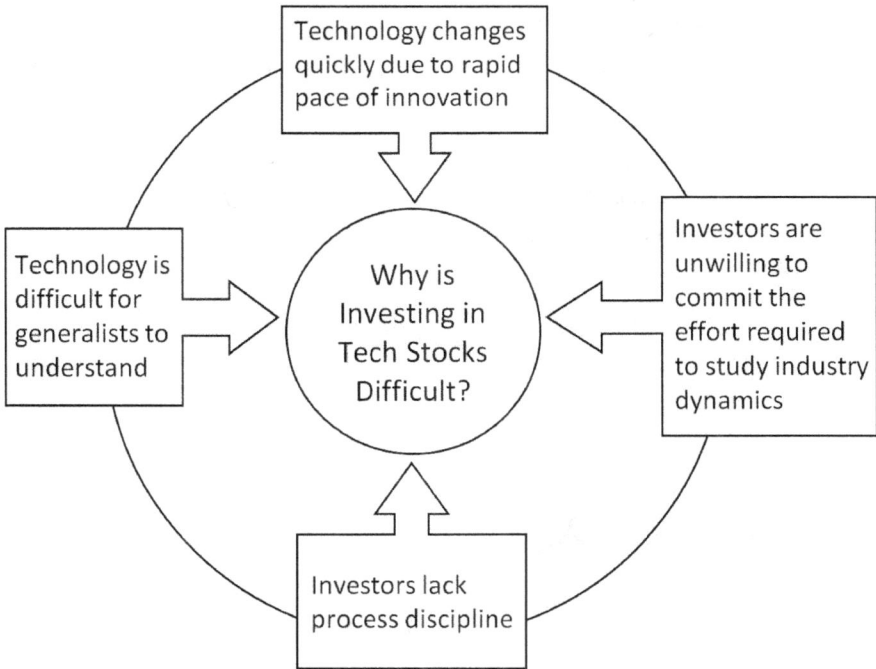

In this chapter I am going to describe my view of the tech industry investment opportunities as of the writing of this book, in early-2016. Much of my work as a Tech Analyst over the last 9 years, was focused on identifying secular industry dynamics such as the ones highlighted below. An understanding of the bigger picture global industry dynamics provides a framework to focus stock selection on companies that are best positioned to win over the longer term, and avoid companies that are likely to be challenged. To be clear, understanding bigger picture trends is not sufficient in and of itself to make investment decisions.

To understand the industry, it is important to imagine what the industry might look like in 3-to-5+ years. Such imagination leads to formation of hypotheses, which can then be tested and refined through data gathering, and interviews with industry experts. Obviously the process of coming up with hypotheses and converting hypotheses to investable ideas is not a quick one. But if done consistently and diligently, such efforts build conviction, which represents a critical element of the "margin of safety" assessment. Ultimately it is this conviction that allows one to confidently buy stocks that are being discarded by the market, often at deeply discounted valuations.

Clearly, it is advantageous to do the required industry and company analysis well in advance of the event(s) that drive target stocks to discount valuations. The graphic below captures my approach to tech investing.

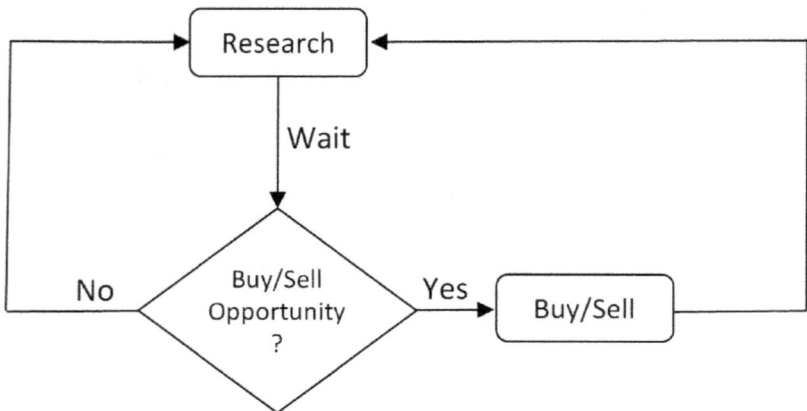

Of course I would never recommend for anyone to invest in an industry, technology, or company simply to participate (perhaps passively) in a trend that one does not fully understand. If you aren't a technologist yourself, there is a good chance that before you hear of a technology trend that it has already been well known to other investors for a period of time, and this likely means it is already priced into individual stocks. Just knowing the buzzwords doesn't mean that you understand how the underlying technology works or what the specific current industry dynamics are. This requires research that needs to be done *before* making an investment. Admittedly I have caught myself getting excited about new technologies, and immediately wanting to make an investment. Thankfully I have been quick to remind myself that this is exactly how big investment mistakes are made. The technical term for this is "chasing" an idea or a stock. Unfortunately this is much too common in the industry.

Knowledge of secular industry dynamics can lead to lucrative investments when you can ascertain that:

1) you understand what the trend is, why it is occurring, and how it impacts the world, and
2) others are either unaware or explicitly disagree with the trend - the latter is preferable, because you can never be sure that others are unaware.

I am including descriptions of several technology trends in this chapter knowing fully well that they will become partially or fully outdated over time, and perhaps give me a chance to revise this book with newer trends later.

Secular Investment Themes – Past, Present, and Future

In the following pages I will discuss five secular industry dynamics – Self-Driving Electric Car, Cloud Infrastructure Growth, Moore's Law Challenges, Transition to Low-Cost Base Station, and Flexible Display. I believe that all of these dynamics are already in play to different extents. Importantly, I think industry changes represented by these dynamics will continue to influence investments in the technology space for the coming years.

Self-Driving Electric Car

This topic is close to my heart because I did research work on autonomous navigation back in graduate school at the University of Minnesota, through projects funded by the Minnesota Department of Transportation, for the safety of snowplows. I have followed progress in this area over the last twenty years. I think we have today a unique confluence of factors that are enabling and accelerating progress in self-driving car technology. I think the most important factor at play is Tesla's success, which has made electric cars a reality, and emboldened large technology companies like Google, Apple, Samsung Electronics and Nvidia to explore expanding their market reach into the car market, in which they have historically had limited if any presence. After all, once you replace the internal combustion engine and transmission with an electric motor powered by batteries, a car starts to look like a computer on wheels. Computers have already been flying airplanes for a long time, so imagining that computers could also drive a car shouldn't be that difficult.

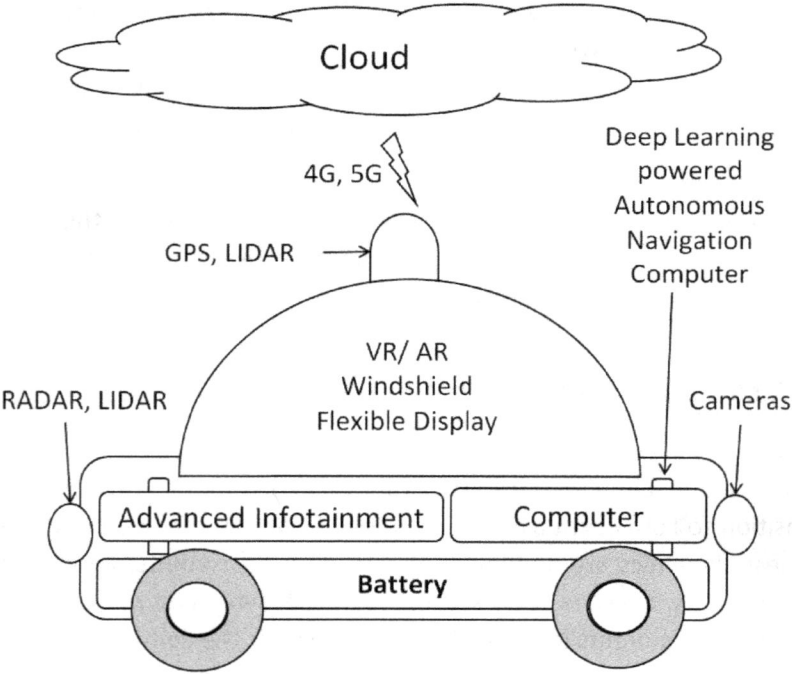

Cloud

4G, 5G

GPS, LIDAR

Deep Learning powered Autonomous Navigation Computer

RADAR, LIDAR

VR/ AR Windshield Flexible Display

Cameras

Advanced Infotainment

Computer

Battery

The chart above illustrates the key ingredients of a self-driving car – most of the ingredients have been available in the market in one form or another for many years if not decades.

Passenger safety and prevention of environmental pollution have both been important factors influencing the automotive market, and self-driving electric cars hold enormous potential to drive solid progress on both fronts. Consequently, governments around the world are likely to cooperate on the policy front, to make appropriate adjustments and accommodations for self-driving electric cars.

From an investment perspective, there are a number of potential opportunities that are being created due to this multi-year secular dynamic – sensors, batteries, deep-learning algorithms and computer technology, and Cloud-based infrastructure to enable autonomous navigation are some examples. If you are not driving your car, then perhaps you want to be productive doing something else, or you want to be entertained while you are being driven around by your car. This represents a potentially large opportunity for advanced infotainment using virtual reality or augmented reality delivered through modern flexible wrap-around OLED displays. If you thought security and privacy of your Smartphone was important, think about the importance of such protections for your car, as it transforms into the ultimate connected mobile device. I also think there will be opportunities to invest in infrastructure supporting a massive ecosystem of connected cars – having "active" elements of infrastructure such as roads, bridges, tunnels, overpasses, parking garages, etc. would enhance inter-vehicle and vehicle-to-infrastructure communications, solidifying the promise of higher passenger and infrastructure safety that self-driving cars represent.

As with any industry that is maturing or has matured, automotive industry incumbents would like to maintain control on the industry's profit pool, assuming that internal combustion engines and mechanical transmissions would provide a solid competitive moat. One way they might have done this in the past is by resisting the transition to electric vehicles – first with hybrids, and then with all-electric cars. It is probably well known that innovation around hybrids was driven by Japanese car makers, while Tesla drove innovation around all-electric cars. Luxury car makers in Europe recognize that they have a chance to self-disrupt by accelerating innovation around self-driving cars, and they are coming around to embrace this dynamic quickly. As the industry transition to all-electric self-driving cars accelerates, existing supply chains for internal combustion engines and transmissions would clearly be impacted.

As of this writing, only a few investment managers had done any meaningful work on the topic of self-driving cars. Needless to say then that the majority of investment managers will be surprised by the changes that they will witness over the coming months and years.

Cloud Infrastructure Growth

As I wrote about self-driving cars, there is a broader industry transition underway toward connected devices – connected home, connected hospitals, connected fitness monitoring, connected oil & gas research, connected supply-chain management, etc. This is also referred to as Internet of Things (IoT), and represents a major driver of growth in Cloud infrastructure, which is at the receiving end of all the data generated by such connected devices. The chart below provides a quick snapshot of multiple changes occurring in Cloud infrastructure as it continues to grow quickly.

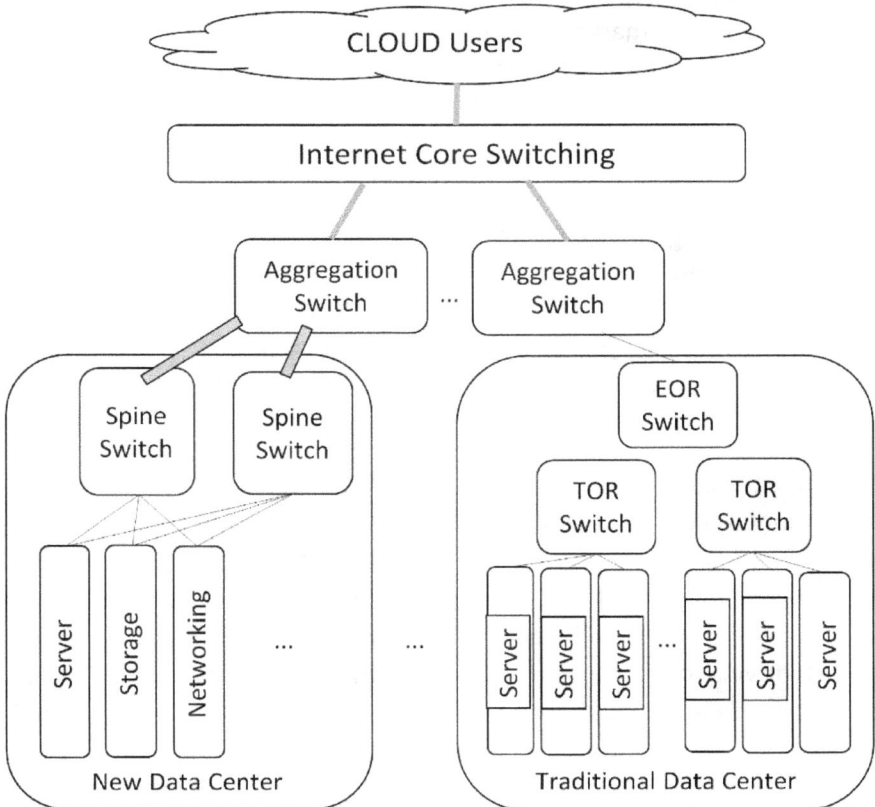

It took me a few months to piece this chart together based on a number of conversations with industry experts (I was also working on many other things over that period). If you are a technologist working in the Cloud space, then the illustration below may seem trivial to you. However, I can assure you that as of this writing, the average investor was unlikely to have heard of the tech terms appearing in the chart below, and would know even less if anything about the functional relationships between the different blocks shown in the chart. Yet such ignorance would hardly stop the average investor from claiming to be actively investing in Cloud infrastructure.

My purpose of drawing the chart was to identify multiple points of changes expected to occur in Cloud infrastructure over the next several years, providing secular opportunities for investments that may not be fully valued by the market, owing to its collective ignorance of underlying technology. As data center hierarchy flattens, it creates points of disruption for Server, Storage, and Networking capabilities. Communication links within and between data centers have to be upgraded to faster speeds, like 100G (100 gigabits per second).

As of this writing, stocks like FB, AMZN, NFLX and GOOG are trading at elevated valuations (P/E NTM >50x) because the average investor is bullish on the growth and disruptive power of Cloud-based software and service business models, even though I might venture to guess that few investors truly understand all the dynamics underlying Cloud growth – the rest are in for the ride for as long as it lasts.

The chart below offers a high level perspective in a user-centric framework. A key premise of the chart is that Cloud infrastructure growth so far has been driven by consumer applications and services, such as Google Maps, Google Search, Gmail, YouTube, Facebook, etc. New services will continue to be added to the Cloud, for new capabilities such as self-driving car, online to offline, virtual reality, etc. As the Cloud advances to deliver ever-increasing scale for a variety of usage models, innovation in the Cloud is occurring at a faster rate, compared to traditional fixed-function, expensive and proprietary enterprise hardware and software. Consequently there is a secular disruptive force generated by Cloud growth (see next chart), and as an investor, you want to be on the correct side of this dynamic to avoid investment losses.

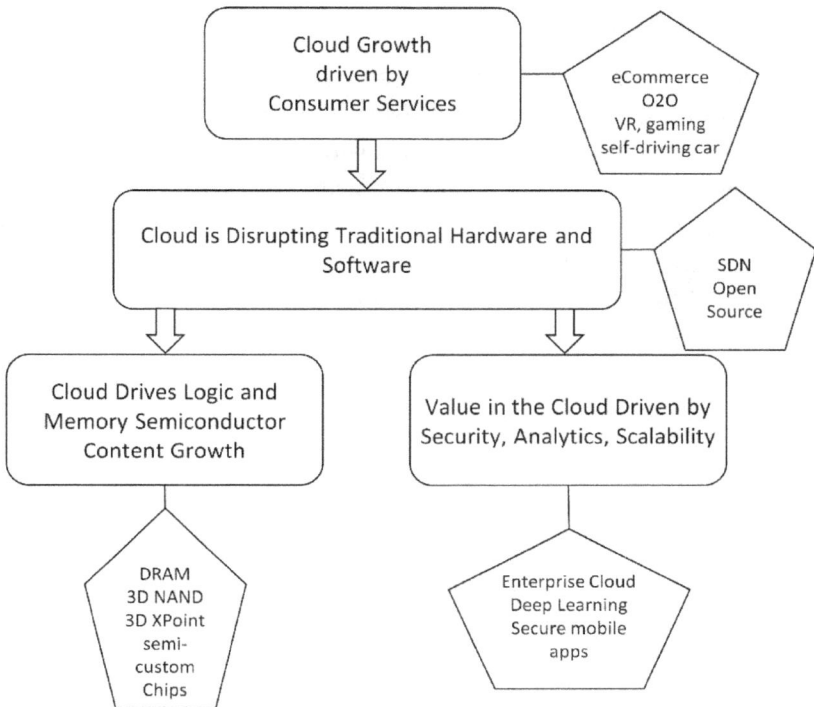

As we discussed back in chapter 4, IBM for example went through a very public exercise of resetting its strategy at least a couple of times, to position itself better to capitalize on Cloud dynamics. Question is, which other companies out there have not yet fessed up to their Cloud-driven problems?

As of this writing, "deep learning" enabled by neural networks and other techniques is emerging as a potent technology powering artificial intelligence. Is it possible that artificial intelligence one day effectively solves the problem of identifying profitable investments?

Moore's Law Challenges

Moore's Law has prevailed in the electronics industry for over fifty years, and predicts that the number of transistors per square inch in integrated circuit chips (IC) would double every 18-to-24 months. This profound dynamic has been a key enabler of the enormous growth we have seen in the electronics industry. Simply put, a transistor is a unit of functionality. This means the more transistors you can pack in a chip, the more capable the chip would be. Electronics industry growth driven by Moore's Law is illustrated in the chart below.

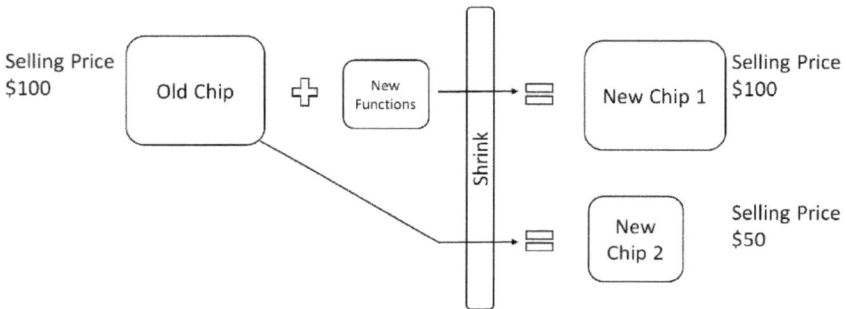

If you have an advanced chip that you sell for $100 today, you can produce a similar sized chip with dramatically more functionality integrated next year (New Chip 1 in the chart), through what is popularly referred to as a "shrink" process. Chip size has been a proxy for chip cost in semiconductors, because chips are printed in volume on circular silicon wafers, 300mm in diameter. The more chips you can print per wafer, the lower the cost of a single chip. By this logic, you can sell your New Chip 1 for $100 next year, delighting your customers, who would happily upgrade to the newer product, given its advanced functionality.

Additionally, you can shrink your existing chip without adding new functionality, to create a lower cost product (New Chip 2 in the chart), which you can sell to new customers at a lower price ($50 in the chart). By doing this, you just expanded your market by segmenting your product to serve more customers who previously couldn't afford your product. If you continue doing this year after year, in theory you can target a progressively increasing customer base with products that continue to advance in capabilities over time.

After more than fifty successful years, the economics of Moore's Law are starting to come under pressure. Equipment needed to shrink chips is either not available for advanced geometries, or has become prohibitively more expensive. This is because semiconductor manufacturing has run into fundamental limitations driven by laws of physics – whether it's the wavelength of light used to print smaller transistors, or the number of electrons available to preserve transistor switching functionality. This is in turn driving changes in how integrated circuit chips are manufactured.

Advanced ICs are increasingly being built with 3-Dimensional device structures (compared to 2D or planar transistors historically), using a different mix of equipment and materials. All of this taken together has created and will create many multi-year secular investment opportunities for patient value investors. This includes investment opportunities in semiconductor devices, semiconductor manufacturing equipment, design service and IP providers, as well as other supply-chain participants. While a few investors with semiconductor industry expertise understand these dynamics, most investors do not. Below I briefly discuss investment implications of this dynamic in a couple of different areas of the industry.

In the most competitive value-added segments of the market, such as Smartphone Application Processor (AP), companies with access to lower cost advanced manufacturing (aka leading-edge, high density) will have an advantage over others that cannot afford to use advanced manufacturing. Integrated Design Manufacturers (IDM) like Intel and Samsung Electronics who both design and manufacture their own logic chips, will be in a position to eke out a cost advantage over competitors that have expertise in design or manufacturing but not both. Of course these companies will still need to execute flawlessly to convert their theoretical advantage to an economic one. On the flip side, competitors like Qualcomm, TSMC, Mediatek, and others would be at risk of being disrupted by Intel and Samsung.

In the commodity memory market for DRAM chips, the implications are different. As the technological ability to deliver economical "shrinks" diminishes, there is higher likelihood of achieving equalization in cost structures across industry participants Samsung, SK hynix and Micron. In an oligopolistic industry with uniform cost structures, there should be little incentive for excess capacity due to fear of mutually assured destruction. Stable or decreasing industry capacity in turn would stabilize both industry and individual company profit pools, making a traditionally volatile commodity market much more investable. Generally speaking I have found investors readily latching on to the "oligopolistic industry" part of the implications without fully understanding why or how cost structure equalization would occur, and how the two are connected.

In the semiconductor manufacturing market, barring a large step function advancement in lithography (aka advanced photo printing), emphasis will continue to shift toward alternative technologies enabling 3D device structures. Companies who provide such alternatives, like Applied Materials and LAM Research, would be well positioned to take share from the old guard, including ASML, Nikon, and KLA-Tencor.

Transition to Low-Cost Base Station

Wireless base stations (BTS) which do signal processing and switching for cell phones, used to be big, expensive, fixed-function boxes costing ~$45K or more just a few years ago. Part of the problem was that these BTS were using expensive components like high-end FPGA, which itself used to cost a few $K. Upgrading such BTS every time there was a change in wireless air interface standard, e.g. from 2G to 3G to 4G, used to be difficult and expensive. The infrastructure has been transitioning to lower cost BTS, using a more optimized architecture. See the illustration below.

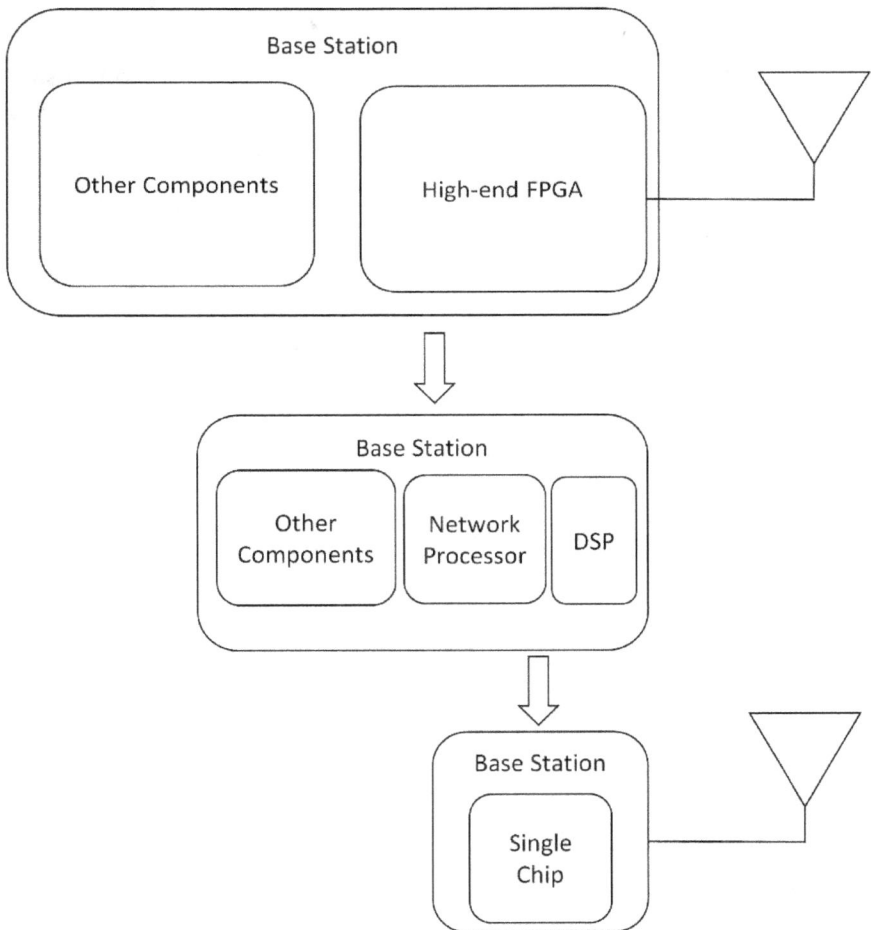

Expensive high-end FPGA are being replaced by a combination of Network Processor and DSP, while other components are also being optimized to lower cost. This has created opportunities for network processors provided by Cavium (NASDAQ: CAVM) in a secular way that investors were oblivious to until well after the dynamic started to play out a few years ago. When I first identified this dynamic in early-2012, company management had still not started talking about this opportunity as a major growth driver for the company. However, over the period that followed, management discussion with investors increasingly shifted toward this dynamic, and CAVM stock appreciated as it got credit for the BTS opportunity.

As of this writing in early-2016, the BTS market is continuing to transition to lower-cost products, with a view to increasingly shift core capabilities into Cloud infrastructure, where it can be managed more efficiently.

Flexible Display

Electronic displays as we know them are changing, and this has broad implications across the industry. Almost everyone is familiar with LCD (Liquid Crystal Display) displays that have been used across many devices for decades. As the need for using thinner, higher-resolution, lower power, and attractive displays continues to grow, the industry is shifting toward a newer type of display called OLED (Organic Light Emitting Diode). Samsung Electronics has been the most prolific user of OLED through Smartphones and Tablets. As of this writing, we are witnessing early stages of another big shift in display technology toward what's referred to as flexible display.

As the term "flexible" suggests, such new displays are built using materials capable of changing shape, such that the whole display can be bent, folded, rolled, or stretched. The images below were reproduced from U.S. Patent Publication # 20140198036 (U.S. Patent Application # US 14/155,935 by Samsung Electronics), and provide a few illustrations of the concept of flexible display.

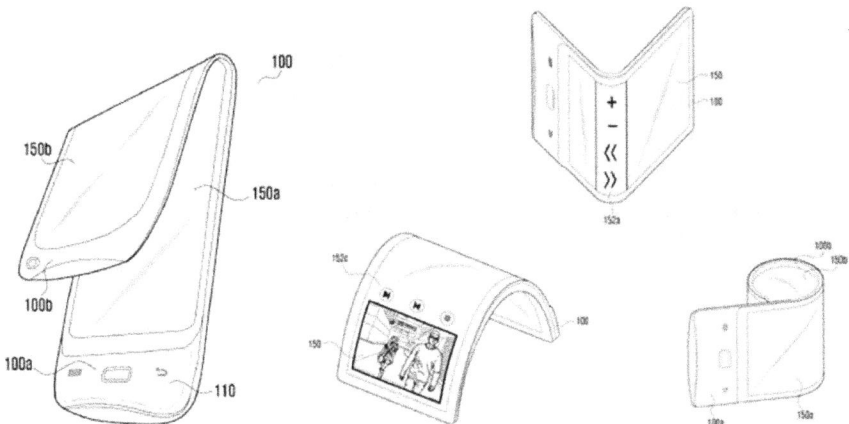

In late-2014 Samsung introduced its first flexible display smartphone called Galaxy Note Edge. Most investors probably ignored it as just another gimmick featuring a marginally useful "edge" display. What is profound about that smartphone and many that have followed it is that they use fully flexible display panels underneath hard cover glass exteriors. Since the phone itself is not flexible and does not change shapes, Samsung's underlying innovation may have gone unnoticed. The next leg of this journey, as you might imagine, is for the hard cover glass to be replaced by a flexible material, such that the whole smartphone is able to change shape.

In addition to potential ramifications for the LCD supply-chain, a transition to flexible display by major industry players like Samsung, LG, and Japan Display, would also create the need for advanced equipment to manufacture such flexible displays. Applied Materials (NASDAQ: AMAT) is the world's largest provider of such display-manufacturing equipment, along with smaller companies like AP Systems based in Korea.

Do you think you are well behaved?

Having spent most of our time on technical skills and processes for company and valuation analyses so far, it is time to shift our attention to the behavioral land mines you have to deal with when it comes to investing. Starting with Chapter 9, in the next three chapters I discuss different types of behavioral issues that routinely crop up in investing. As with many things in life, knowing that you have a problem increases your probability of addressing the problem.

Chapter 9 – INVESTORS BEHAVING BADLY

As human beings we have certain inherent deficiencies that can limit our investment success. While it may not be possible to eliminate all such deficiencies to become perfectly unemotional investors, we can certainly try to be more conscious of our behavioral pitfalls. Such awareness can help avoid or mitigate costly investing mistakes, as well as perhaps profit from mistakes made by others. In this chapter I am going to point out some of the most common behavioral traits that I have experienced and/or noticed first hand. There are great books written on the subject, and I have included references to some of those books at the beginning of this book. I have also used this section to point out certain behaviors and actions that institutional investors frequently introduce into the stock market, with a view to profiting from such events as an individual investor or investment manager.

Over Confidence

Impatience

Excess Trading

Loss Aversion

Behavior Problems

Confirmation Bias

Anchoring

Window Dressing

Availability Bias

Impatience

I am writing about impatience before other more "exotic" behavioral issues because I have noticed impatience as being the single biggest issue with my own investment behavior. Impatience could manifest itself in a variety of ways. For me, I find myself most impatient when adding to position for a high-conviction idea. I am worried that others will magically figure out everything I know instantaneously, and the stock will rise quickly, without allowing me to build a big enough position to get the most value from my idea. In that sense I guess impatience is probably connected with greed for me. This is where I have found adherence to a specific buying discipline extremely effective – it could be something simple like "don't buy the next lot until the price drops at least 10% from your current cost basis". Whatever it is, it is always helpful to have it written down. Until it is written down, it is but just a figment of your imagination, easily forgotten when market pressure builds and misbehavior kicks in.

On a broader basis impatience is probably the easiest to understand and relate to, whether it is about struggling to hold on to investments long enough to allow your thesis to play out, or difficulty in resisting unnecessary action when things change quickly around you. Patience is critically important for being a successful value investor, to make sure stocks are not purchased until prices are depressed enough into value territory and offer a substantial margin of safety.

Excessive Trading

Some stocks seem to trade within relatively predictable ranges, and become easy trading targets. Investors form a habit of buying such stocks near the low ends of their ranges and selling them higher. Making money this way isn't bad in itself, but the issue is the impact it has on the investor's overall psychology and behavior with other stocks. Once you get used to making "easy money" and trading frequently, you start to think very highly of your capabilities as a stock picker, and this over-confidence interferes with analysis of securities, especially within a value framework. An activity that ideally should be limited to a specific set of trading stocks, starts to spill over to other stocks, and very soon, portfolio churn increases, and process discipline gets thrown out of the window.

Confirmation Bias

Everyone likes to be right, and it would be nice to be right all the time. But investors must accept one irrefutable fact of investing – you are going to be wrong more often than you'd like to be. Confirmation bias involves seeking data or information with the singular goal to prove your investment thesis is correct. This involves discarding data or information that might disprove your thesis. Unfortunately, this means you are consciously or unconsciously subscribing to "herd mentality", and shutting out the very signals that can help you avoid losses.

Value investors take the opposite approach, seeking out data or information that might disprove their thesis, instead of looking for everyone to agree with them. Through this process they often uncover potential mistakes or gaps in their investment theses, long before they risk losing invested capital. I'll say this – it takes a different kind of emotional stability, determination, tolerance and resilience to continually bombard yourself with opposite views to test your assumptions. Not everyone will find this enjoyable or sustainable, and that's what separates value investors from the rest of them.

Over Confidence

It is easy to confuse your investment success with your ability rather than pure luck, such as when the entire market is rising due to quantitative easing, among other things. Unless you consistently followed a regimented process for selecting your investments, and your process has worked consistently under different time periods, including periods during which the market as a whole was not appreciating, then perhaps you have a legitimate ability to identify good investments. If you can't articulate to yourself why your investments were successful, then perhaps it was pure luck – not a bad thing to have!

Other forms of over-confidence occur when you put too much emphasis on pieces of data or information that are bound to be imprecise or inaccurate, especially within the context of a technology industry dynamic that you don't fully understand, for example.

Anchoring

Most assets do not have fixed or static values attached to them, and inability to estimate their values precisely is what makes investing difficult. Yet some people refuse to acknowledge the world has changed or is changing around them, and hold on tightly to prior beliefs – whether this is investment frameworks or playbooks they might be familiar with, or values of various types of assets, especially assets they might have purchased.

Framing, which is a powerful technique for negotiation, unsurprisingly can also influence your view of a set of facts. For example, risk management may get more attention when framed as "insurance". Anchoring to certain forms of presentation can detract from core messages locked in underlying data.

Loss aversion

No one likes to take losses on investments, but sometimes you have to, usually to avoid further losses. If new information that becomes available after you make an investment, suggests that your investment thesis is no longer valid, then there should be no reason to hold onto your investment. This is even more important if your investment has already incurred a loss. Yet investors often fail to take action that would generate a smaller loss to avoid a potentially larger one later in time.

Lack of process discipline is usually an underlying factor for the inaction. If there wasn't a clear investment thesis supporting your position in the first place, then it's not going to be clear whether you should hold onto your position after it has significantly declined in value.

Good Company vs. Good Stock

Investors like to buy stocks of companies they "know" and "trust" and "love". While it may be emotionally comforting to invest in this fashion, it isn't much different from gambling in your favorite casino. Your individual preferences in terms of the products you chose to use, while certainly important to you, may not be representative of the choices made by other customers of such products around the world. You may have ignored competing products, or a bigger shift in the underlying way of accomplishing tasks served by such products. You may also not have a good understanding of profitability or other business or technology dynamics surrounding such products. Last but not least, you may not have paid attention to valuation, which may be elevated because other investors are thinking exactly like you are.

As I described earlier, I value my first-hand experience with new products, particularly when my findings are out of consensus. Having a view of what products you like or don't like cannot be stopped; but using such a bias to guide your investments may not be appropriate, particularly if it involves turning a blind eye to other process elements described in this book.

Availability Bias

It is human nature to pay more attention to information that is more recent, even if it might be incomplete, or an outlier that is not necessarily representative of normalized conditions. Market participants recognize this implicitly or explicitly, and try to take advantage of it. With the exception of a few companies that take the high road on this, you will find company managements actively engaging with investors intra-quarter, sometimes even through "quiet periods". Company representatives hope their availability for discussions serves to stabilize the market's view of the stock, even though they are usually not really sharing material new information or updates.

Window Dressing

"Window Dressing" is a term that refers to cosmetic changes that fund managers make near the end of the quarter, to give the impression that they are holding or not holding certain stocks, which fund-investors might care about as they evaluate future investments. While such actions do little to influence the fund's recent performance, fund managers hope such actions might help them mask mistakes made intra-quarter, and give the appearance of holding winning stocks, or not holding losing stocks.

Window dressing is a symptom of two things we have discussed in this book:

1) fund manager incompetence, and

2) excessive focus on the short term.

Trading on Material Non-Public Information (MNPI)

There are always some that like to cheat on exams, or in managing portfolios, knowingly or unknowingly, as the case might be. When it comes to technology stocks, there are far too many investors that know little or nothing about the businesses underlying those stocks. One day when SanDisk (NASDAQ: SNDK) shares were falling sharply, I got a call from a well-respected mutual fund portfolio manager asking "what is N-A-N-D?" If you are familiar with SanDisk, the company is one of the world's largest manufacturers of NAND Flash Memory, which is used in a range of digital storage applications like Smartphones, Cameras, USB drives, etc. This "poor" PM had probably become an investor in SNDK, because someone told him that SNDK was a play on Apple (NASDAQ: AAPL). That was in fact the entirety of his investment thesis in SNDK, and with shares of SNDK trading down double digits, he was understandably panic-stricken, trying to figure out if he should sell the shares and exit his position. I asked him to hold on to his SNDK position, explaining that there were others like him that were selling with little basis for their actions, than fear.

Since few are willing to or able to invest resources in fundamental equity research, the motivation to cheat by looking for MNPI to gain an edge over others isn't difficult to understand. It's a potential shortcut that is also illegal. Buyside analysts and PMs receive countless phone calls daily from sellside analysts and other information brokers, each with their own "differentiated" views on a security. One way that some people differentiate their views, is by claiming they are calling from the parking lot of the company they are calling about – emphasizing the timeliness of their call immediately following acquisition of new information, and the urgency of their actionable intelligence. Buyside investors routinely encourage their sellside counterparts, and other industry sources to call them with such just in time intelligence, before they call anyone else.

Some investors think they have special skills for extracting MNPI from company management, through advanced techniques for questioning and reading body language. Such investors routinely demand private meetings with company management, when attending conferences hosted by the sellside.

Machine Trading

With all such behavioral risks at play, it may seem tempting to just unplug and let your computer do trading automatically for you – if that was even possible. Turns out that it is, and a number of active managers are using it, but perhaps not for the reasons you think. The big after-market up or down spikes that you see in stock prices typically following company earnings beats or misses are one example of hyperactive machine trading. Another type of machine trading comes more broadly from macro or quantitative strategies that automatically execute a series of pre-calculated trades that don't necessarily have much to do with actual company fundamentals. As of writing this book, the world is witnessing an unusual correlation between stock market prices and the price of oil. Do you think lower oil prices are bad for every company or business in the world? What if lower oil prices were driven by excess supply of oil and had nothing to do with overall global demand for commodities?

Why Value Investing is Hard

In a lot of cases you are going to be buying value stocks while they are still being ignored, if not actively discarded by the market – this is often called "catching a falling knife" amongst professionals, for good reason – see the next chart. Unless you are buying in a very large fund, in very large chunks, chances are that your buying has very little if any effect on the market price of the stock. In other words, quite likely, you are going to find the value of your recent purchase decline soon after acquiring it. Question is, for how long can you stomach seeing the value of your holdings decline, and by how much, before it stabilizes and starts to move up? And are you confident that you will use such declines to build position as originally planned, or exit your position at a loss instead?

"Catching a Falling Knife"

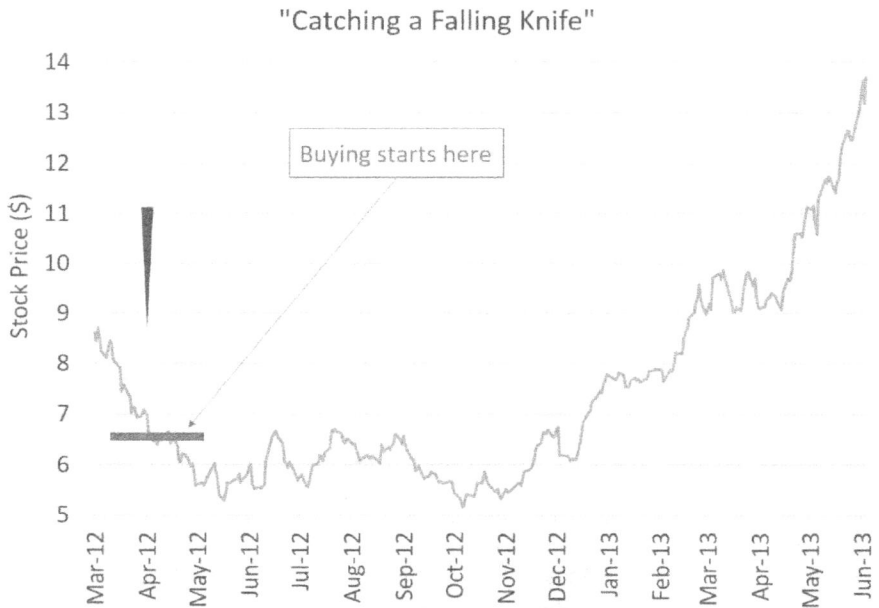

Even if you like the core idea of value investing, and have a desire to put it in action (not everyone does), actually implementing it is fraught with challenges – from doing the hard work needed to identify undervalued securities, to building conviction, to then following through with buy/sell disciplines to ensure you maximize investment returns. How much work you do, and how much conviction you build ahead of acquiring a position in a value stock determines how well your psychology might hold up as you stand against the herd, facing declines in value while you continue to accumulate the stock.

Standing against the herd can by psychologically draining, not necessarily because the value of your portfolio is shrinking, but because new bearish arguments echoing in the market may uncover a scenario you hadn't considered, and stands to render your thesis invalid. If your thesis is invalidated, you will not only not have a reason to buy more stock, but may in fact have to exit your position at a loss. Even if you are not bothered by the idea of looking like an idiot as your portfolio shrinks, while others are merrily chasing popular ideas, you are still bound to be concerned about potentially being wrong. This is precisely where margin of safety helps, by making sure you haven't overpaid for the stock, even if your bigger thesis is wrong.

Value investing is a difficult balancing act – you want to keep your eyes and ears open for new ideas surrounding your investment just enough to make sure you are not falling out of touch with your core thesis (this is especially important in technology stocks); but you don't want to overdo this, because if you do, you will be consumed by the herd preaching the other side of your thesis. You literally have to work hard to preserve your sanity, shut out the noise, and stay focused on fundamentals and data rather than emotion. If you can't relate to what I am describing, try visiting a blog like SeekingAlpha.com and observe the member commentary on articles that challenge the consensus view on any stock. Depending on the particular stock and the level of fanaticism associated with it, you are likely to find that the mob doesn't want to hear an opposite view. The herd will thrash the author of an article that suggests that reality might be a little different than what the consensus view prescribes. If you have your emotions in balance (most people don't), you can learn a lot from such herd reactions, identify where the pain points are, and exactly where the herd could be wrong.

Case Study: Micron

Look at MU's stock chart over last 3 years and ask yourself this question – did Micron's intrinsic value really change multifold (from ~$6 to $35, and then to ~$10) over the last 3 years? Up and down? As of writing of this book, MU is among the top-10 most shorted stocks listed on the NASDAQ, with the company trading below P/B of 1x, at <50% of the replacement cost of its factories – this is how herd mentality works, particularly in tech stocks, and represents an enormous opportunity for tech-savvy value investors to profit from.

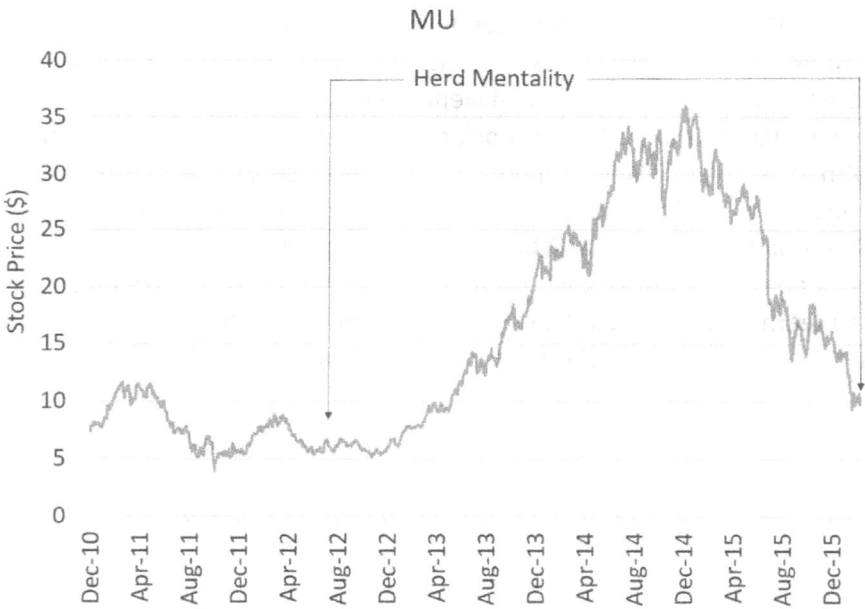

Case Study: IBM

If you strongly believe the industry and company work we looked at in the IBM case study in Chapter 4, and the broader Cloud market dynamics illustrated in Chapter 8, then as a value investor you have to be willing to go against the herd and start buying IBM stock as shown in the chart below, knowing fully well that the stock could continue to decline (you know that it did). You will never know in advance how much a stock will decline before it turns; because as we saw in Chapter 3, stock prices may not necessarily be driven by a view of fundamentals. Furthermore, you will also need to be prepared to (happily) keep buying as the stock falls to new lows, to average down your cost basis.

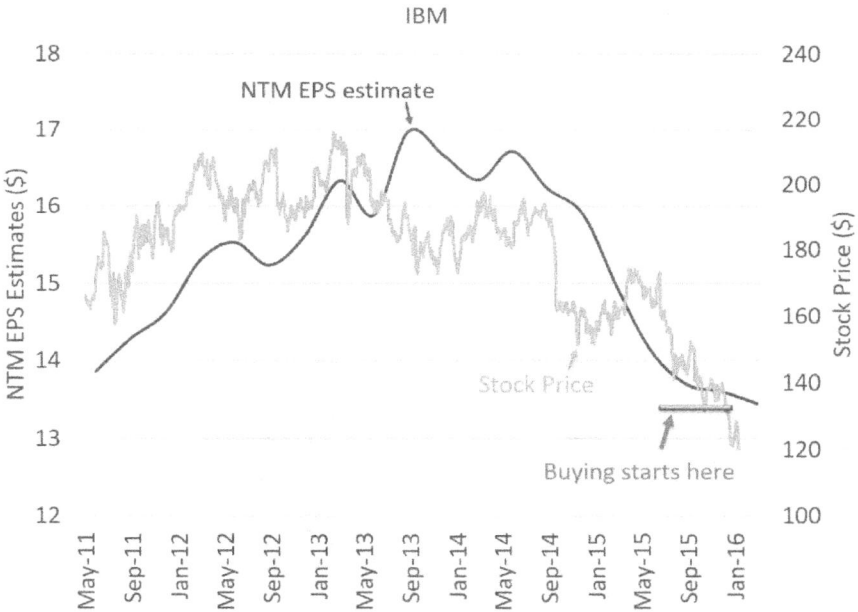

I hope it is clear that this is not really a specific (or complete) pitch to buy IBM, as much as it is an example of behavior that is common for value investors, and an explanation for why value investing can be difficult to execute even though it may sound great in theory. Investors have to try hard not to be their own worst enemies when it comes to investing.

Look in the mirror

"The investor's chief problem – and even his worst enemy – is likely to be himself" – Benjamin Graham, in The Intelligent Investor.

I have presented a critical view of market participants in this chapter and in this book for your benefit. But before you get carried away and start faulting every fund manager out there, let me first ask you a question - if you find that your chosen, trusted fund manager is underperforming the market over the last month, quarter, year, or two years, are you going to: 1) rush to withdraw assets from this fund manager, and dish them out to another manager who outperformed over those periods? Or 2) are you going to have faith in her, maintain your longer-term investment horizon, and let her do her job maintaining her longer-term focus? (Hint: correct answer is #2).

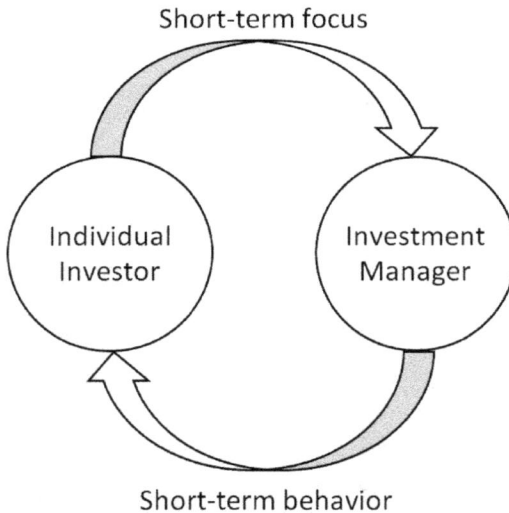

Short-term focus

Individual Investor

Investment Manager

Short-term behavior

If you picked #1, I'm afraid you along with others like you just took responsibility for the majority of the bad things occurring in financial markets, as virtually every market participant scrambles to deliver short-term outperformance to vie for your assets.

Here's another question that I think would be worth for you to ponder on - Would you prefer to 1) accept calculated/planned discomfort in terms of

156

short-term underperformance upfront, knowing that your investments are on the right track for the longer term, Or 2) would you rather defer such discomfort indefinitely knowing that it is bound to strike suddenly without warning, may last a while, and may erase substantially all of the short-term gains that you might be enjoying? (Hint: correct answer is #1).

You will recognize that these are simple questions, but not necessarily easy to answer, even if the right answer is kept in front of you. These questions get to the core of the problem faced by the investment management industry overall. The core problem compounds into a much bigger problem when it comes to investing in specialized sectors like Technology, where a short-term focus combined with limited or no domain knowledge of the industry together form a recipe for investing disaster that few managers can side-step.

The good news I think is that the problem is solvable, at least for you, the individual investor. The solution involves taking a longer-term view of your investments, and trusting yourself and your chosen independent investment manager to her job. Perhaps you will appreciate this better after a comparison of active vs. passive investing, in Chapter 10.

Chapter 10 – ACTIVE VS. PASSIVE INVESTING

This is a heavily debated topic, for good reason – many trillions of dollars of investment capital is at stake, and the active management industry which captures the majority of management fees surely does not want to see its earnings get truncated. I am certainly not an expert on this topic because I have not analyzed all the data, in part because it has been difficult to get my hands on good data. But based on the work I have done, I do have a perspective on what might be best for the individual investor, and this is also how I have been managing my own assets. This chapter offers practical frameworks for the individual investor to think about her own needs and preferences.

Warren Buffet's famous advice to individual investors would be to put 90% of their assets in a broad market low-cost stock index fund (e.g. S&P 500 ETF) and to put the remainder in short-term government bonds. His principal objective of course is to help his followers protect their assets from 1) massive losses that could result from investing actively on their own without the proper skillset or behavior control, and 2) exorbitant investment management fees that would eat into investment returns without delivering better-than-market returns. Obviously however, if you can find an investment manager like Warren Bullet, then letting him or her manage your investments could lead to a better outcome – i.e. higher returns while undertaking lower risk, as compared to investing passively as suggested in Buffet's advice.

Understanding the Zero-Sum Game – Some Useful Frameworks

From a mathematical standpoint, the market as a whole is a zero-sum game – i.e. outperformers are counterbalanced by underperformers, the net of which is performance in line with the market. The larger an individual fund (e.g. mutual fund, hedge fund) gets, the harder it becomes for that fund to beat the market. It is worth pointing out that for an investment fund to perform in line with the market, it has to actually beat the market by the amount of the management fees being charged. E.g. if you are paying a management fee of 200 bps, then the underlying fund has to consistently beat the market by 200 bps, just to deliver in line performance. But you are probably not paying a 200 bps management fee just to perform roughly in line with the market, because that can be accomplished for much lower fees (~20 bps) through a low-cost index ETF, and the 180 bps spread in fees can compound to a substantial performance difference over long periods of time. No wonder then that over the last several years the industry has seen a major flight of investment capital away from active funds to passive funds and ETFs.

There are a couple of complicating factors – when the market is appreciating quickly, as was the case over the last several years since the financial crisis of 2008, active managers find it difficult to beat the market, because it becomes harder to pick "winning stocks". Active managers tend to perform better than the market when the market is in decline, as it affords them a bigger opportunity to put their stock selection skills to work. Over longer periods of time then whether active funds beat the market or not becomes a function of relative durations and magnitudes of the market's appreciation or depreciation – this is hardly a variable that the active management industry can control on its own.

Active managers employ a large number of very smart and skilled analysts, who routinely identify good companies to invest in. Smaller funds are able to take concentrated positions to extract full value from such "alpha generating" ideas identified through deep fundamental research. Larger funds on the other hand find it harder to run a portfolio with just a handful of concentrated positions, and force themselves to diversify their holdings. This means that good ideas identified by the good analysts don't get to be big enough investment positions, under the premise of "managing risk", i.e. not wanting to display shorter-term periods of potential underperformance in favor of longer-term outperformance. Diversifying a portfolio by definition pulls it closer in composition to the broader market, hence structurally reducing the fund's outperformance relative to the market. And it is not hard to imagine that "closet indexing" by the larger funds drowns out strong returns by smaller investment managers to make the industry as a whole look worse.

The net takeaway from this is the same as what we have discussed throughout this book – individual investors need to identify their needs and goals, and then work with trusted investment managers to come up with an investment plan that would bring them closer to their goals. Blindly putting your money in a mutual fund because it was rated five stars by a rating agency due to the fund's good relative performance in the most recent period(s), unfortunately doesn't qualify as smart personal investing behavior from my standpoint. A slightly better alternative might be to invest in a fund managed by an investment manager that you have studied and know enough about to trust with your assets. How many individual investors have the ability to follow or study a specific investment manager to determine if her style is acceptable? Perhaps low-cost ETFs start to look really attractive at this point.

ETFs – Virtually Without Problems

If you are investing in a well-known market index (e.g. S&P 500), through a low-cost ETF (expense ratio of ~20 bps), with a long-term (i.e. multi-year) horizon, with recurring contributions made on a recurring basis, then you are probably on the right track – or at least you might be on the same track as Warren Buffet's assets invested for the benefit of his family, after he is gone. ETFs have been around for over two decades, and seem to have done a satisfactory job of tracking the major indices they are modeled after. Except for temporary pricing glitches observed occasionally, ETFs seem to have been free from major liquidity or index tracking problems. It's worth mentioning that ETF index-tracking performance seems to vary across different indices, and it is possible to have ETFs with higher tracking errors for certain indices such as those representing international stocks.

Even in the case of bonds, there appear to be legitimate reasons to consider buying a bond ETF rather than a comparable bond mutual fund. One such reason might be a structural problem that bond mutual funds face during significant unexpected redemptions, due to fundamental pricing inefficiencies of bonds – this is effectively what led well-known Third Avenue Management of New York to freeze its bond mutual fund upon facing severe redemptions recently. However, I am personally not fully convinced that a bond ETF would necessarily completely sidestep problems arising from concentrated severe redemptions.

Given the overall convenience and efficiency of ETFs, the investment selection problem could be reduced to an asset allocation question – what portion of your assets do you want invested in a stock ETF vs. bonds or cash. While the super-long-term investor with a large amount of excess assets may be content with a fixed allocation that mechanically directs majority of the investments toward stock ETF(s) and the remainder toward bonds, the average investor may not appreciate such a strategy during interim periods where the market as a whole declines in value significantly. While passively investing with ETFs may be a wise choice over mutual funds, it would be structurally incapable of protecting assets during periods of market turmoil – an outcome that may not be acceptable to a large portion of investors. For such investors, having a trusted investment manager might be the only wise solution. The chart below illustrates the different options.

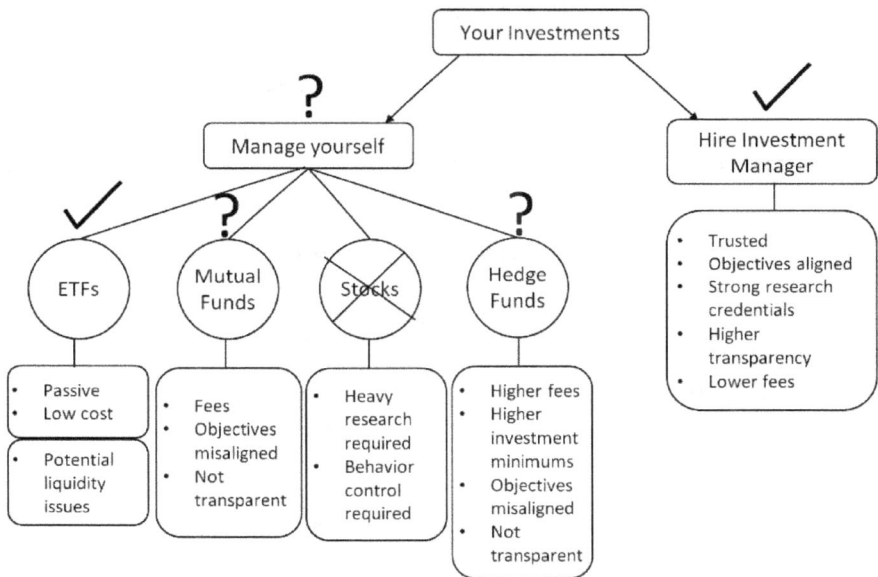

Passive Investing Strategies

The investment world is full of various types of strategies. Below I am briefly describing a couple of relatively well known strategies. Keep in mind that every strategy comes with its own advantages and disadvantages. So I would not recommend pursuing any particular strategy on your own, without the help of a trusted investment professional.

Dollar-cost Averaging. In dollar cost averaging, a fixed amount of money is invested in the market at regular intervals, regardless of what market prices are. By doing so, this approach tries to minimize market timing risk by preventing large sums of money from being invested at the top of the market for example. But conversely, this strategy on a standalone basis also prevents large sums of money from being invested at market bottoms.

Value Averaging. In a value averaging approach, investments are made periodically with the objective of bringing the portfolio balance to a predetermined level, established upfront using a mathematical formula. Investment actions are carried out regardless of market fluctuations, which are automatically accounted for as the portfolio is "topped off" or "creamed off" when each adjustment is made. Unlike dollar cost averaging, this approach may also drive partial liquidation/withdrawal of investments from a portfolio, if the value of the portfolio has risen above the predetermined level for a given period.

Portfolio Management – Diversification doesn't necessarily lower risk!

Researching and picking good individual investments is a big part of portfolio management, but certainly not all of it. Portfolio management includes other important tasks like trading, liquidity management, and risk management. Risk management includes a combination of hedging and diversification.

Diversification is the concept of holding a variety of different types of securities, to lower overall portfolio risk. Value investors think of diversification differently in that they aren't as concerned with volatility reduction which is one mathematical byproduct of diversification, but rather about understanding differences in risks posed by individual investments – those are two different things, as we discussed earlier in this book. For example, if I hold Micron, Intel, and IBM stocks, then I would have concentrated exposure to Cloud Infrastructure spending, and may need to find something to offset some of the Cloud risk. Or I may decide that I in fact do want concentrated Cloud exposure for a period of time. On the other hand, some of the cyclical high-fixed-cost semiconductor risk intrinsic to Micron and Intel would be diversified by owning IBM, which generates majority of its revenues from software and services. Clearly this is very different from the mathematical consequence of lower combined variance of the portfolio due to beneficial cross-covariance effects of its constituents.

Estimated Time to Research One Company

The table below should give you some idea of the time it takes to execute different research activities required to analyze a given company.

Research Task	Time
Earnings call: listen to one company call or read transcript and organize notes	90 min
Update one company model after earnings (quarterly update)	1-2 hrs
Review one 10K/10Q	1-2 hrs
Build Historical Company Model	10-40 hrs
Attend company analyst day	8-10 hrs
Attend industry conference	8-40 hrs
Build Industry Model	10-40 hrs
Call or meeting with industry expert	0.5-2 hrs
Topical analysis	1-20 hrs
Write research report	1-40 hrs

Depending on the size of the company, the complexity of its operational history, competitive and supply chain dynamics within the industry, and ease of access to information, it could take more or less time than that indicated by the ranges in the table. Assuming good access to information (even if for a fee), building quantitative models is probably the easiest part of the research effort, only requiring relatively basic knowledge of accounting, and process discipline to make sure that excel-based model work is error-free. Industry analysis on the other hand is much harder, and activities related to conference attendances, and interviewing industry experts may need to be repeated multiple times to form a high-confidence qualitative view of the industry. Furthermore, a number of activities represented in the table need to be repeated regularly, usually at least once every quarter, to stay current with the company's financial updates and make sure the over-arching investment thesis is still valid. Even if you are investing with a long-term horizon as recommended in this book, ignoring quarterly and other timely updates is hardly advisable, particularly for technology stocks for which fundamentals can change quickly. Your goal is to identify and correct investment mistakes sooner rather than later.

The huge amount of effort involved in researching individual stocks is the main reason why I think individual investors should avoid investing in individual stocks (i.e. active investing), except on a recreational basis (i.e. if no other superior means of recreation are available), with at most a limited and insignificant amount of capital put at risk. Desire to contribute actively to your investment portfolio by identifying specific stocks based on your knowledge of technology industry dynamics, is probably much better accomplished through an aspirational engagement model that I propose in Chapter 13. First lets discuss how stock selection mistakes are made, in Chapter 11.

Chapter 11 – DEALING WITH INVESTMENT MISTAKES

Nobody likes to make mistakes, but reality is that mistakes do happen from time to time, and are guaranteed to occur in the world of investing. So the question is not whether you will make mistakes, but rather how you will deal with mistakes. A lot of the discussion in this chapter is probably not unique to investing, but certainly more important to the world of investing, where the basis of most transactions is rooted in client trust. It takes a long time to build trust, but just a moment to lose it. Since I spent a lot of time discussing my investment process and how or why it was successful earlier in the book, I thought it necessary to add this chapter about investment mistakes, so that I could come clean about at least a couple of mistakes I know I have made.

Does your favorite mutual fund or hedge fund make investment mistakes? Are those mistakes and their resolution communicated to you? If you are paying a management fee for someone to manage your investments, shouldn't they provide sufficient transparency for you to know how your investment manager is making investment decisions? Does reading a quarterly or yearly newsletter satisfy all your curiosities about how your assets are being managed? How does your investment manager determine she has made a mistake? What's your investment manager's process for rectifying mistakes?

I recently asked a well-known portfolio manager at a well-reputed mutual fund that prides itself in its fundamental analysis-driven investing process, what his process was to determine whether he had made a mistake with a particular stock. His answer – "the market tells us that we made a mistake". Do you think that answer is consistent with his stated strategy of fundamental analysis, based on everything we discussed in this book so far? Unless he is holding a stock for a short-term trade, a fundamentals-driven manager should not be looking to the market to tell him whether he picked the right stock. For a fundamentals-driven manager, determination of a stock selection error would occur only upon learning that he made a mistake in analyzing underlying business fundamentals, which he should be tracking carefully. At least he was honest, or perhaps he didn't have a chance to think about his answer. Either way, his response is certainly not unique, and a number of honest and well-known portfolio managers will probably answer the same way. Perhaps this serves to highlight the tension that such managers live with every day – to advertise to their clients that the fund is fundamentals-driven, but accept the reality that fund managers look to the market for answers far too often than they should.

In this chapter I am going to discuss a couple of the mistakes I have made in my investment analyses over the years, and what I have learnt from them.

RMBS case study – Samsung contract reset

I initiated coverage of RMBS in December 2013 with a Buy rating because I was convinced that a positive inflection in Samsung's DRAM revenues would translate into commensurately positive inflection in Rambus' DRAM-related royalties from Samsung. After having analyzed the DRAM industry in detail, and estimating a high correlation between Samsung's DRAM revenues and Rambus' DRAM-related royalties from Samsung, I was confident that significant earnings upside was likely for RMBS. In early-January 2014, just a few weeks after my initiation of coverage, Rambus announced that Samsung had reset its contract with Rambus to a lower rate of royalties. With my primary investment thesis on the stock having proven wrong by an unexpected contract reset, I downgraded the stock to a Hold rating on the news.

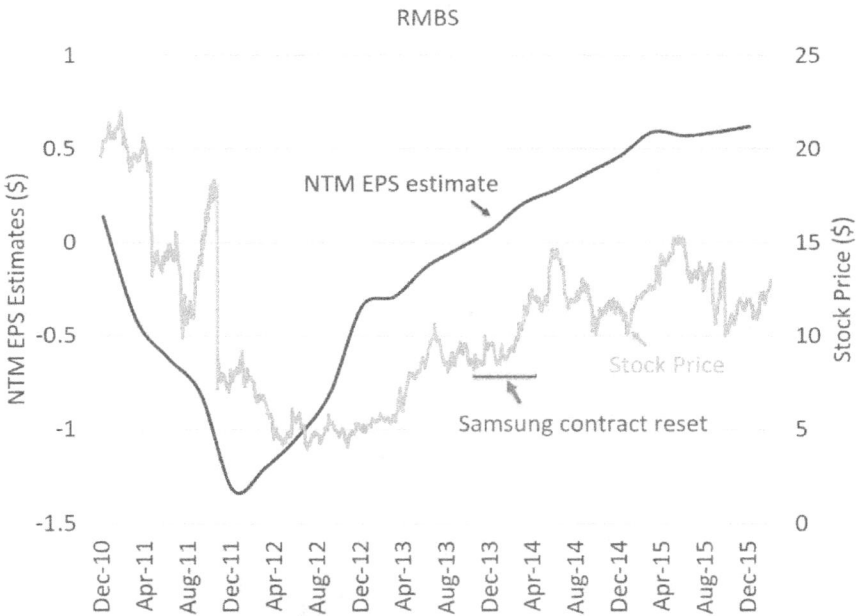

The problem here was the binary nature of the fundamentals driving the Buy recommendation. Even though there was nothing wrong with my analysis, there wasn't enough of a margin of safety in the Buy recommendation, given that it was singularly driven by DRAM upside, assuming Samsung would continue to pay royalties at the existing rate. The Rambus case study underscored the need to have a multi-factor investment thesis, such that if one of the factors didn't play out as expected, you could still hold on to the stock for other reasons. That unfortunately was not the framework I had used for Rambus.

The next case study illustrates that even after having a multi-factor investment thesis, it is possible to be wrong on a stock, again due to no specific fault of your own except perhaps that you didn't anticipate the level of expectations already baked into the stock before deciding to buy it.

AMAT case study – TEL merger termination

I recommended Applied Materials (NASDAQ: AMAT) with a Buy rating starting in early-2014, based on a multi-factor secular thesis, which included a positive inflection due to AMAT's planned merger with Tokyo Electron (TEL). Following several delays, AMAT finally announced in early 2015 that it had terminated its merger agreement with TEL due to regulatory hurdles in closing the merger. Following announcement of termination of its TEL merger, AMAT stock took a big hit, from the mid-$20s to the mid-$teens. The mistake I made here was not accounting for a sufficient margin of safety with my Buy recommendation.

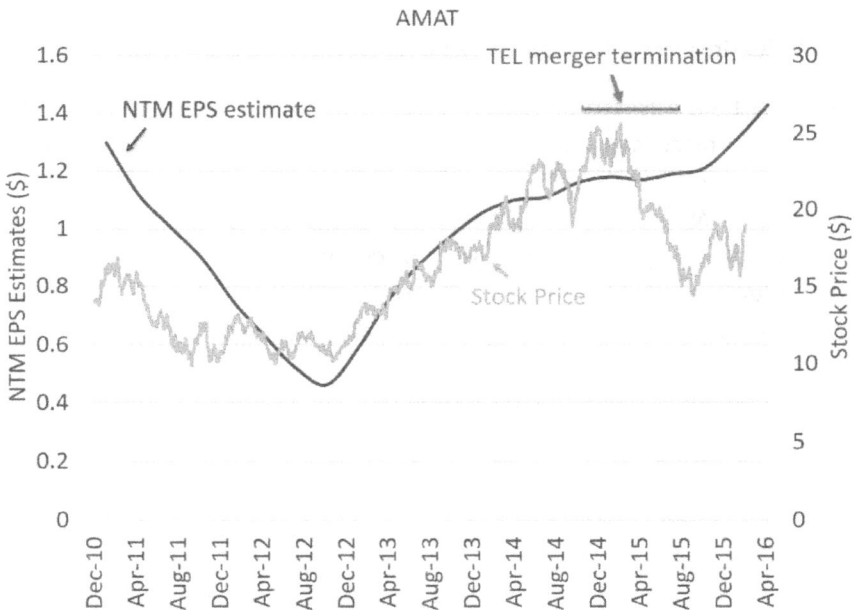

AMAT

If you look at the red line (NTM EPS estimate) in the chart above, you can interpret that standalone fundamentals for AMAT had performed solidly as of this writing, and this suggests that non-merger-related positive secular factors included in my Buy thesis played out more or less as expected. Not properly assessing how much merger-related euphoria was already baked into the stock price, was the mistake here. Since early-2014, AMAT had consistently traded at a NTM P/E multiple of ~18x, i.e. roughly in line with its peer group. In other words, AMAT was not trading at a significant valuation discount, and had not significantly underperformed in the period leading to my Buy recommendation. If you compare these factors to the framework I presented in Chapter 6, you will find that the margin of safety considerations were not satisfactorily met. Treating the TEL-merger as a high-probability scenario was the culprit.

As it turns out, as of this writing, secular fundamentals for AMAT I thought were still positive, virtually for the same reasons that they were positive in early 2014 (ex-TEL). With the stock having underperformed due to the TEL-merger debacle, the stock carried a higher margin of safety trading in the mid-$teens, though the stock's valuation multiple remained healthy.

Why Value Investing in Technology is Difficult for Generalists

The chart below is a modified version of a chart you saw in Chapter 3 where we discussed what drives stock prices. This chart dissects "Company Fundamentals" into "Business Model" and "Industry Dynamics". While a generalist value investor would be capable of understanding the business model of a technology company, she may not fully understand the influence that various industry dynamics might have on the company's business model. This affects the process of assessing intrinsic value, and introduces risk in the investment process, making the process difficult to execute successfully.

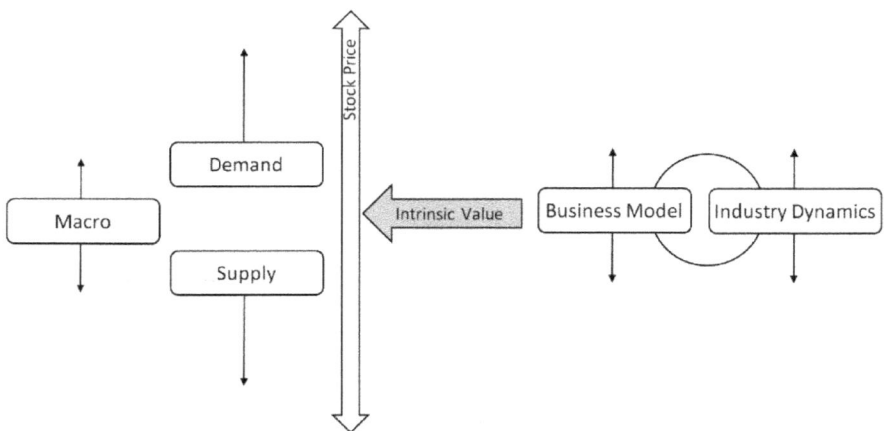

As I have said throughout this book, if you are investing in technology stocks, but don't think you have a strong understanding of underlying technology industry dynamics, then I'm afraid you might be misleading yourself or your investors. Furthermore, your chosen investment strategy is then most definitely not "fundamentals-driven", but rather driven by some other short-term oriented trading strategy that may or may not have a popular name – like "technical trading" or "swing trading" or "momentum trading".

Next in Chapter 12, I provide a framework to think about different types of information and data that are available to a technology investor, and discuss my best practices for using such information.

Chapter 12 – SOURCES OF INFORMATION

The most useful pieces of any analysis, are the data supporting it. One way to process new information is to distill it down to its two constituents – data and sentiment/opinion. Opinions without supporting data or evidence should either be deemed virtually worthless, or taken with extreme skepticism, unless the author is a practicing industry expert on the topic.

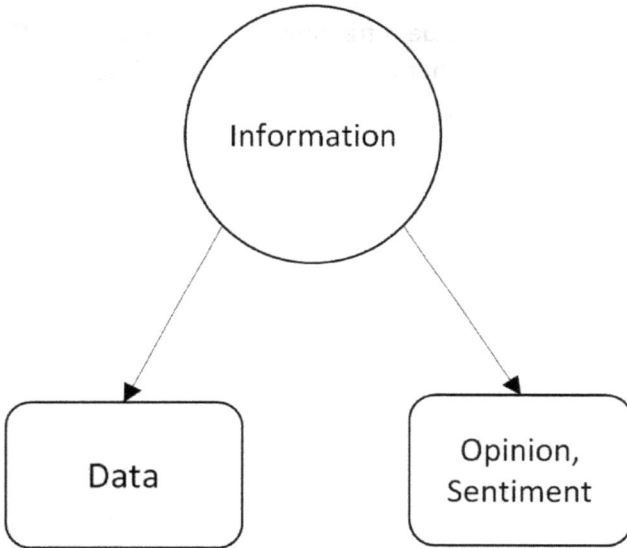

```
                    ┌──────────────┐
                    │              │
                    │ Information  │
                    │              │
                    └──────────────┘
                     /            \
            ┌──────────┐      ┌──────────┐
            │          │      │ Opinion, │
            │   Data   │      │ Sentiment│
            │          │      │          │
            └──────────┘      └──────────┘
```

News, Magazines, and other media

In case you hadn't noticed, media reports are frequently biased, particularly when it comes to reporting about stocks. The Wall Street Journal, Barron's, Marketwatch, Financial Times, New York Times, and countless other media around the world consistently make an effort to pass judgment on company earnings results, and stock reactions following earnings results, implying that the journalists following these companies or stocks have developed financial expertise, and their opinions should therefore be trusted by their average reader.

Everyone wants to be a financial advisor, but few are held accountable for their recommendations. Of course I am not suggesting that journalists are not intelligent or trustworthy people – quite the opposite in fact – journalists I know are extremely smart and savvy about assimilating topical information. Unfortunately however it is easy for the average investor to get carried away by a provocative news headline, regardless of the facts underneath. Having an opinion or a bias is certainly not wrong - everyone is entitled to his or her own views and beliefs. However, when one or more journalists' opinions which may or may not be based on facts/data, and may or may not be technically accurate, have the power to influence the thinking of their less-informed individual readers, then such readers need to be careful and cognizant of the pitfalls of putting too much emphasis on such news articles while making investment decisions.

I have learnt that the best way to process news articles is to consider new data being presented (if any), and take into account the direction of implied sentiment (positive or negative) on the company, technology, or stock. Having knowledge of investor sentiment can be useful in understanding a stock's valuation. Conversely, the worst way to process news articles would be to immediately trade stocks based on the direction of commentary in the articles.

The next chart captures sources of different types of information that an equity research analyst needs to process continuously. Items in the column on the right hand side of the chart are typically paid services used by investment professionals, whereas items on the left are available to the common public free of charge.

Company website Investor Relations section ⟹	10K/10Q Press releases Presentations Webcasts Basic model	Factset, CapitalIQ, Sentieo, Bloomberg ... ⟹	Advanced data services and charting
MarketWatch Yahoo/Google Finance ⟹	Basic Stock info Stock performance charts Sell-side consensus estimates News	Brokers: Etrade, Charles Schwab, ... ⟹	Research reports
Seeking Alpha ⟹	Earnings Call transcripts Research articles	Market Research: Gartner, Counterpoint, InSpectrum ... ⟹	Industry data and analysis
Morningstar ⟹	Historical financial model (Excel) Historical Valuation	Expert Networks: GLG, SumZero, ... ⟹	Industry insight, channel checks

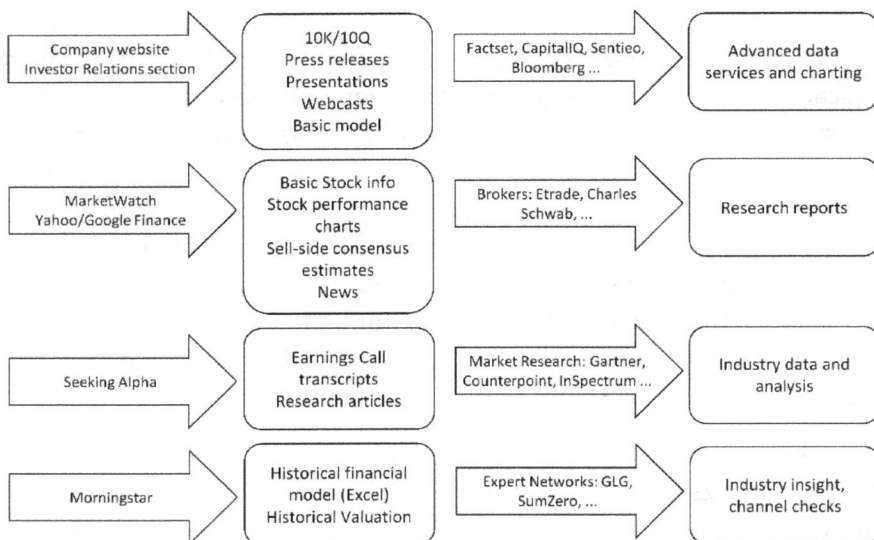

Sellside analyst reports

Ideally sellside reports should give you the most up-to-date data and analysis of company fundamentals, to allow you to make your own investment decisions, but unfortunately they seldom do. As we discussed earlier, buy/sell/hold ratings can be useful, but don't have to be, if you focus on data and analysis instead of opinions. Yet many investors get emotionally fixated on the ratings, language and price targets in these reports, instead of focusing on fundamental analysis.

Sellside research gets a bad name for a few reasons, all of which I think are legitimate – 1) there is too much collective focus on short-term tactical data points and earnings analysis, which have limited relevance without a coherent big-picture thesis, 2) big model and rating changes around earnings events introduces volatility in earnings estimates and spreads confusion about longer term fundamentals and intrinsic value, 3) there is minimal focus if any on industry analysis of secular trends, and how a particular company fits within that trend, short term and longer term, 4) organizational challenges discourage thinking out of the box to apply different techniques to uncover and communicate insight. The result is more or less insanity, bred by sellside participants following the same process as everyone else, but each expecting to magically produce highly differentiated results.

While industry expertise through academic training and work experience at one or more companies in the industry should I think be a prerequisite for the sellside analyst job, it certainly isn't. As a result, with a few exceptions, what you get is effectively a collection of talking heads, who appear to be chasing popularity among their clients, rather than investment alpha generation. Need I say that such behavior is directly or indirectly motivated by how sellside analysts are compensated?

Given all of this, I think where sellside reports can be most helpful is when the analyst is initiating coverage on a company or a group of companies within a sub-sector of the industry. This could be due to an IPO, or part of the analyst's strategic coverage. The utility of such initiation reports would be primarily in their collection and analysis of relevant industry trends and data, rather than their ultimate buy/sell/hold recommendations. Another useful element that the sellside can help with is company models. Instead of building your own models from scratch, it can be more efficient or faster to start from a high quality sellside model to base your own analysis and forecasts on. Never forget to do your own spot checks to ascertain adequate data quality before you lean too far into using a sellside model.

At this point in the book I have covered all the pieces that I believe are involved in analyzing an investment in a tech stock. In Chapter 13 I propose a model for investment management specifically for technology investors to take advantage of industry knowledge, with a view to generate better investment returns compared to the average investor.

Chapter 13 – ASPIRATIONAL IDEAS FOR INVESTMENT MANAGEMENT

As we have discussed throughout this book, achieving higher investment success (or even different results) compared to the average investor fundamentally requires doing things differently. I am laying out my vision for a new kind of investment management partnership that puts clients first, leverages client ideas and insight, and provides a dramatically higher level of visibility and transparency into the investment process for clients. I don't know if some or all of my ideas described here have already been put into action by existing investment managers; regardless I want to share my aspirations as an investment manager, to start a discussion with potential clients. The focus here again will be on the technology investor, though clearly these ideas could be applied more broadly. I think the cool thing about investing is that you almost never have to be secretive about your investment strategies – you can rest assured that even if you are excited about your potentially breakthrough ideas, others are unlikely to follow you until after you are very successful; and by that time, hopefully, you have innovated to the next level of ideas or process advantage. There are also often times, when you want others to copy your ideas, because that can accelerate your investment returns. What I wonder about then, as I am sure you do, is why a number of existing investment managers are so secretive about what they do? What special techniques are they using to generate their "alpha" that they don't want others to know about?

Integrating Idea Generation from Clients

When it comes to the technology space, no one knows everything, and there is value in harnessing the unknown – whether it is an obscure but valuable technology, or a new disruptive high-tech product, or something else. Engineers and other professionals in the technology industry have deep knowledge and insight about their respective fields of work. Even if they can't (and shouldn't) share everything they know, primarily due to confidentiality agreements with their employers, their technology training and industry experience gives them unique insight that can contribute meaningfully toward their investment manager forming a more informed view of the industry.

Having a compliant process to provide a conduit for such industry experts to share their ideas freely without the risk or appearance of insider trading, is critical for the long term success of any such effort. Expert networks today try to accomplish some of this, but in a disconnected fashion, by making it transactional and data point oriented. To be fair, that's their business model – that's how expert networks get paid, when their clients exchange specific (hopefully non-MNPI) information of value. My vision is to build on those ideas to create a framework of connected industry insights that can be "open-sourced", and made freely and readily available to the firm's followers – existing and potential clients, perhaps even competitors. Client identities of course would be held confidential at all times.

You may be familiar with investment clubs. The idea is generally for investment enthusiasts to group together and present ideas to each other for peer review. Perhaps the ideas are acted upon individually by group members in terms of establishing or taking down positions in their portfolios, but that is not strictly required by the club. What I have in mind is again a superset of activities that might be found in an investment club.

I must acknowledge the existence of two specific communities that I have been impressed with – one is SumZero Buyside, and the other is Seeking Alpha. Each has a different focus. SumZero Buyside is exclusive to buyside investment professionals, who are encouraged to regularly post stock pitches, which are then reviewed and commented upon by other members. This generates good discussion, as any investment idea should. It is also useful to start recruitment-related dialog. Seeking Alpha on the other hand is open to the common public. Many of the members appear to be successful independent investors, and/or technology experts as well. Seeking Alpha has become a great resource for investment information, not the least of which is thoughtful articles published by its members. I know there are at least a few professional buyside investors that have started following Seeking Alpha.

The chart below illustrates my vision of a potentially disruptive investment management process that if implemented correctly, could function as a highly productive investment partnership ecosystem for technology investors. As with any financial services industry process, application of appropriate compliance best practices would be key in ensuring smooth operations.

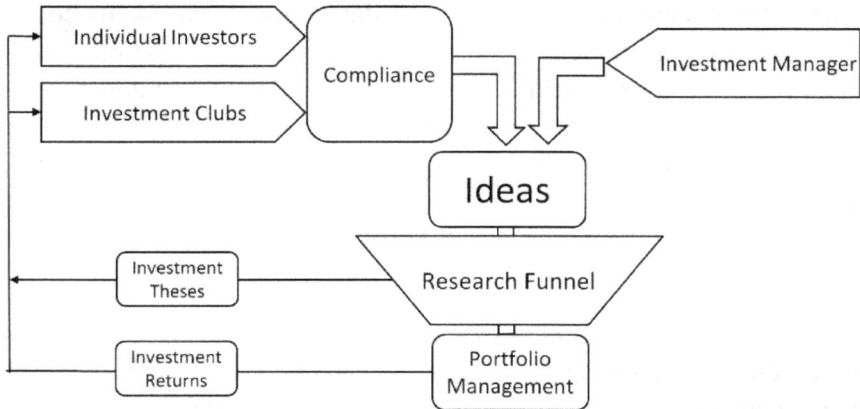

In addition to having a good chance of generating better-than-average investment returns, the process illustrated above would also contribute toward increased transparency and education for all participating parties. Sharing investment theses for specific investments under ownership would serve not just as an element of transparency, but also as an element of process discipline that encourages the investment manager to stay current on her investments relative to her investment theses. In fact the sharing of investment theses could be accomplished independent of integrating individual investor input for idea generation. When it comes to providing transparency, it is worth noting that independent investment managers managing separate accounts technically can provide more transparency compared to a mutual fund or hedge fund for example, because clients who the separate accounts belong to can if they so desire, actively track investments in their accounts as and when changes are made. Mutual funds or hedge funds on the other hand file their reports quarterly, and don't provide much transparency into their thought processes.

Certain types of technology industry professionals, like investment bankers, consultants and lawyers would have to be excluded from

178

participating in the idea generation process discussed above. Such professionals are almost always bound by heavily restrictive non-disclosure agreements with their technology company clients, and the risk of tripping NDAs far exceeds any investment benefit that could potentially be generated from incorporating their insights.

It is worth emphasizing that the process idea described here assumes that individual investors participating in the "idea generation" process have already been granted freedom by their employers or other business interests, to trade freely in securities that their investment manager may invest in on their behalf. Additionally the compliance process highlighted in the diagram would serve to explicitly exclude commentary or insight about specific companies that such individual investors might be employed by, while allowing a discussion of broader industry trends.

As of this writing, the financial services industry had become extremely sensitive to topics pertaining to insider trading, and rightfully so. The process ideas introduced in this chapter are being presented with an assumption that their implementation in any form would at all times seek to be fully compliant with financial industry standards of appropriate behavior, as well as applicable laws. In other words, the process innovation discussed here isn't an attempt to thwart compliance, but rather to embrace it while maximizing both investment returns and transparency, in a way that current industry practitioners on average are not pursuing, for reasons that I think have little to do with compliance.

Being Different Where it Counts

As you may have gathered from reading this book, I am a big fan of challenging the status quo, the consensus view, and the established process, in favor of exploring alternatives that I believe have potential to drive better results. I was very lucky to have had the chance to do things differently as a sellside equity research analyst – I took a value approach to analyzing technology stocks, I focused on longer-term fundamentals, I focused on analyzing the technology industry in ways that I didn't see others doing, and I let the strength and quality of my research drive my engagements with my buyside clients, instead of harassing my clients with unnecessary and incessant phone calls bearing nothing more than tactical short-term trading data points. My experience and performance have reinforced my beliefs, and I feel fortunate to have a research platform from which I can aspire to drive better results in investment management for technology investors.

Appendices

In the four appendices that follow, I provide an overview of various information gathering, organizing, and analysis tools that a technology investor is likely to find useful. While I would be generally supportive of readers of this book taking advantage of the tools and services highlighted, I would encourage you to keep in mind two things: 1) my positive experience with some of the services was based on my relationships with principals at those companies, and your experience may be different; and 2) as of the writing of this book I had not received any monetary reward from the companies appearing in the appendices, beyond their generous provision of data for the purpose of inclusion in this book.

APPENDIX 1 – Harnessing the Power of Microsoft OneNote

I thought a book about investing in technology would be incomplete without talking about how to leverage technology to become a better research analyst. Collecting, processing, and organizing data and information is core to research, and the ability to manage this efficiently can make a big difference in the productivity of an analyst. Conversely, inability to quickly recall critical information on demand can dramatically slow down the research process. The chart below lists the many capabilities of OneNote, all of which I routinely use.

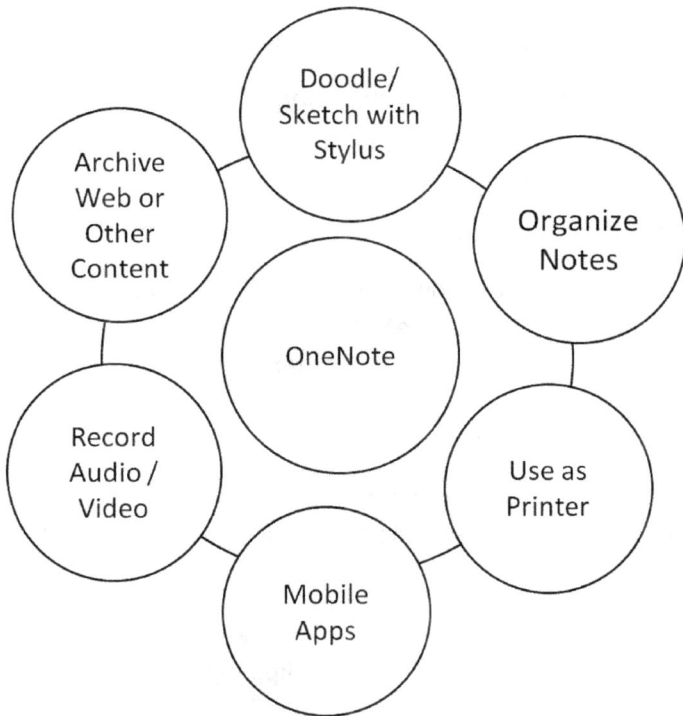

I have used Microsoft OneNote for over ten years, and feel comfortable recommending it as an indispensable tool for a research analyst. OneNote used to be provided as part of the Microsoft Office bundle, but recently Microsoft appears to have decided to distribute OneNote separately for free — a great step forward, if true. Below I describe how I have used OneNote. Almost all the capabilities described below are provided across a broad range of Windows, Android, and iOS devices.

Powerful organizer for notes and more

OneNote provides many ways to take notes, with or without real-time transcription — i.e. handwriting recognition. I think what differentiates OneNote from anything else out there is its powerful organization capabilities. OneNote in essence creates its own virtual file system, allowing you to create individual notebooks, sections, and pages for different types of notes. You can organize all of your notes from within OneNote, and all the changes are sync'ed with OneDrive continuously — you never have to hit the "Save" button.

Importantly, OneNote comes with a potent search algorithm that can search across all notebooks at once, including text embedded within graphics, and certain audio recordings.

Archiving articles or other web content, and document scans

There are four ways that I know of, to do such archiving. The first way is to print a webpage directly to OneNote. When you install OneNote, it also simultaneously installs a OneNote printer, which can be used to print various items directly into OneNote. This almost completely eliminates the need to print on paper.

The second way is to do a good old-fashioned copy and paste. You can grab an entire webpage using <CTRL> + C, and do a <CTRL> + V in a OneNote page.

The third way to grab content is to do screen grabs. OneNote makes it extremely easy to neatly take screen clippings. You can set up a key combination like "Windows + S" to immediately launch a snipping tool that allows you to grab on-screen content from any website or app you might be working in. You can then paste it into OneNote easily with a <CTRL> + V.

The fourth way is to scan a physical document directly into a OneNote page. The input device could be a flatbed scanner, or a smartphone camera.

Doodling or Sketching Ideas and Block Diagrams

The next chart is an example of a chart used in this book, from when it was first conceived in OneNote as a sketch. OneNote has supported the use of a stylus for writing or drawing, for as long as I can remember. This makes it easy to doodle or capture ideas in a free form fashion, to be refined later. The best part of it is having all such doodles in one place, available for easy recall, rather than having to hunt for a physical sketchbook to find or reproduce a sketch drawn on paper.

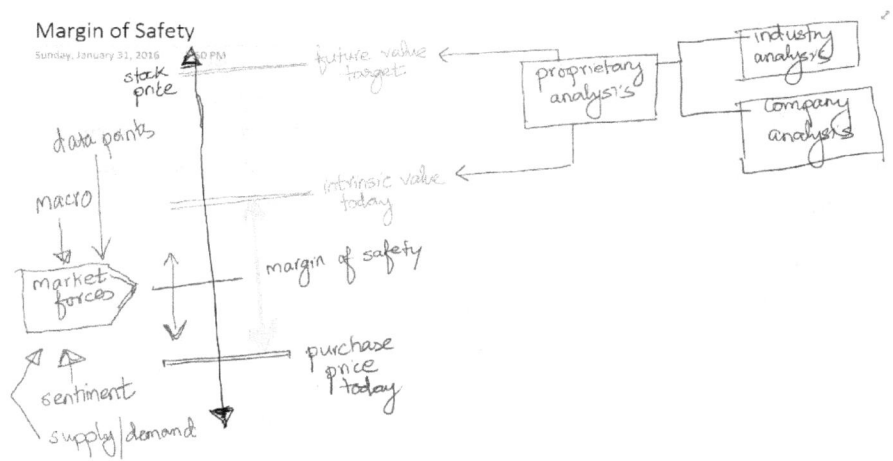

Margin of Safety
Sunday, January 31, 2016

Accessing notes from mobile devices

I have found OneNote's Cloud-based sync function to be top-notch. Whether you are collaborating with yourself across multiple devices, or with others, through shared notebooks, OneNote makes it easy to keep your content together and synchronized. I have used OneNote on Windows, Android, and iOS, and have found it to work well. The best and most comprehensive OneNote experience I think still requires a Windows

PC, though I think it probably works just as well on a Mac. Some of the organization functions, as well as "print to OneNote" functions were still missing in Android and iOS versions of OneNote as of this writing.

Recording audio

I have used audio recordings during presentations, while simultaneously typing notes. OneNote is uniquely able to index the text that you type to locations within the audio recording, to make it easy to review specific portions of the recording rather than having to listen to the whole thing every time.

Alternatives to OneNote

Beyond OneNote, the only other note-taking application I have used is Samsung's S Note, which is available on Samsung devices which feature an integrated stylus (Samsung's Note Series of devices like Galaxy Note 8.0, Galaxy Note Edge, etc.). I have been impressed with S Note's capabilities, particularly when used with Samsung's integrated stylus. Where S Note lacked as of this writing I think was in its ability to organize notes, and make notes easily searchable like OneNote does. Over time I see no reason why S Note wouldn't be able to catch up to OneNote.

I know there are others who like to use EverNote; and from all the reviews I have read, EverNote appears to be just as good as OneNote. As of this writing, Apple had recently introduced its iPad Pro, which came with an optional stylus. After finally legitimizing the free-form note-taking model by creating Apple Pencil, perhaps Apple will over time provide a comparably capable note-taking alternative to OneNote – I frankly don't see the need for one, given OneNote already works on iOS devices, as well as Android devices.

APPENDIX 2 – An Overview of Sentieo

Sentieo is a research workflow solution underpinned by deep search technology. As former hedge fund analysts, Sentieo's principals understand the challenge of digging through an inhuman amount of information to find the key data that makes or breaks an investment thesis. Sentieo meets this challenge by maintaining a comprehensive index of all financial documents and disclosures and then overlays its semantic search and natural language processing (NLP) technology to enable users to quickly find and process key information.

Once users find key information, Sentieo's workflow and sharing features allow seamless highlighting, annotation and collaboration in text and tables. Sentieo's research notebook offers light touch research management to allow analysts to organize and develop their ideas while allowing PMs to monitor and influence the ongoing research process. Sentieo's mobile and iPad apps ensure that analysts and PMs have seamless access to all financial content and notebook data on the go and even in offline environments. Sentieo's Excel plugin, Chrome browser plugin, and API extend the platform to everywhere analysts do their work.

As of this writing Sentieo was used by the buyside and sellside at over 40 firms with over $500B in AUM. The average user spent 2-3 hours per week on the platform and reported saving at least that much time weekly. Sentieo had a team of 70 including 40 engineers and has offices in San Francisco, New York, New Delhi and Berlin.

Highlighted Features

Deep semantic search with Natural Language Processing technology and financial synonym dictionary.

Time Series – create 5-10Y of historical quarterly tables from within any table in Sentieo with only a few clicks, instead of having to go through 20+ individual documents. Full auditing capability to understand how all time-series data are sourced.

One click highlighting, annotation and citation of documents. Seamless integration with Sentieo Research Notebook.

Excel export and Excel plugin.

Compare Documents with Redlining. Xray mode enables you to see how numbers have changed from previous filings.

Document Search

The fastest and most powerful way to read and do research in documents. Sentieo creates a comprehensive document index of all key documents and then offers you powerful linguistic search algorithms to instantly find exactly what you are looking for. With seamless linkage to the Sentieo Notebook and Mobile Apps, Sentieo makes taking notes, collaborating in documents and accessing them on the go a snap as well.

Sentieo's Realtime Datasets Include: Global Company Filings (SEC and International), Corporate Event Transcripts from Thomson Reuters, Press Releases from News Wire Services, Company PDF presentations scrapped from 3,000+ IR sites, Tweets and Web-based News Content.

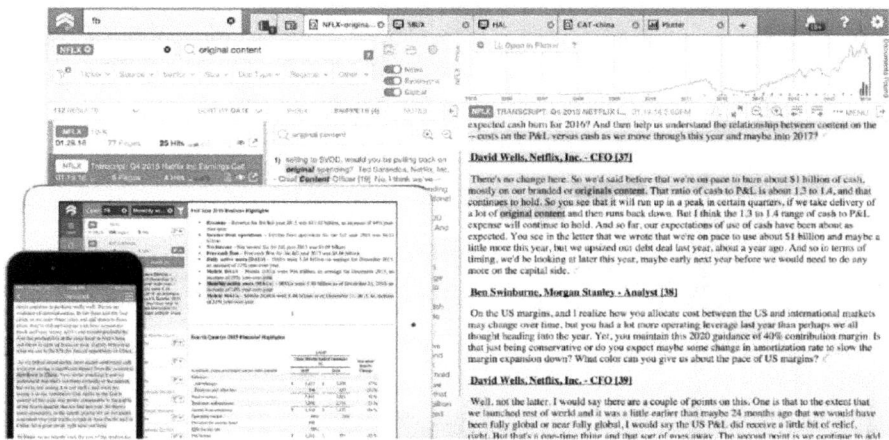

Example Use Case # 1 - Idea generation through open ended searches:
Who is exposed to China? Who is discussing an unexpected slowdown or strategic alternatives?

Example Use Case # 2 - Follow searches and get alerts on new content:
Follow AAPL repurchase to get an alert every time AAPL mentions the word repurchase.

Research Notebook

Sentieo's Evernote-style Cloud Notebook automatically gathers all your highlights, notes, and annotations in Sentieo documents for easy search, recall and sharing of content. Easily add your own meeting notes or idea thesis content and email or upload external content.

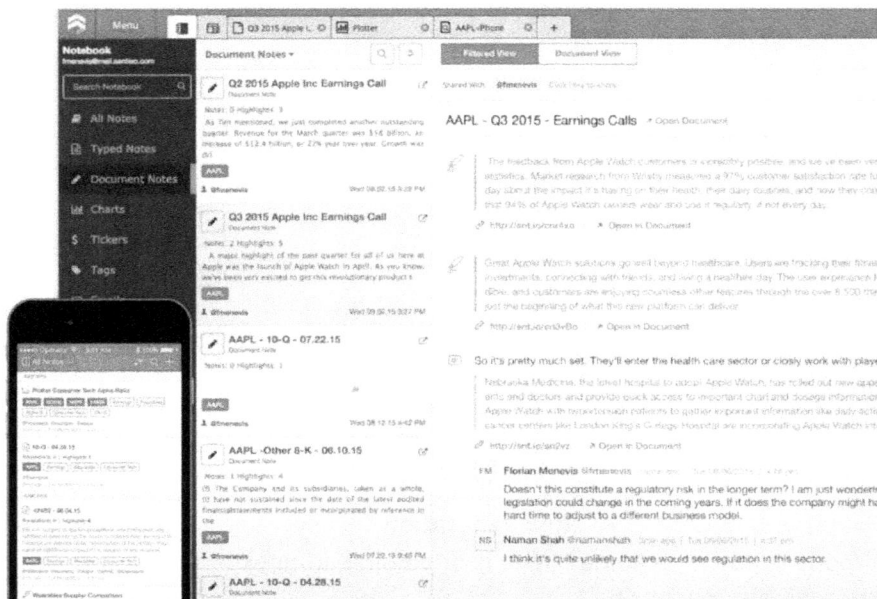

Sentieo Notebook features powerful sharing and workgroup features that ensure your team is always aware of your latest thinking and work. Research Notebook is available across desktop, mobile platforms and iPad, and features seamless integration and instant syncing with Evernote and OneNote. Chrome browser extension web-clipper can be used to save web content and articles in your Sentieo Notebook. Sentieo also provide a forwarding address to email new content into the Notebook.

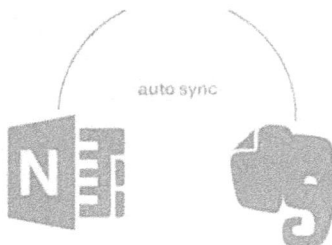

auto sync

Mobile + iPad

Sentieo's iPhone, Android, and iPad apps offer the most powerful apps on the market. Never miss a beat when you are out of the office with full document search, highlighting and annotation, Sentieo Notebook access, detailed financial models/estimates and push notifications for new documents and price moves.

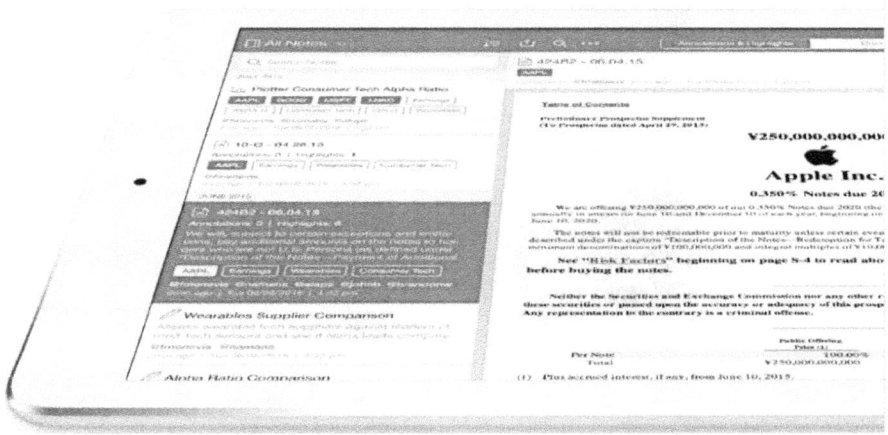

Sentieo's iPad app is the ideal way to read and annotate documents wherever you are. With Sentieo's unique sync, they take your interest list of tickers and locally cache all the key document and financial content to your iPad. That way even if you don't have internet access on a plane or a train, you can read, search and highlight all the documents you care about, with all of this work syncing seamlessly when you next connect to the internet.

Alerts Engine

With a dead simple interface to follow companies and a seamless alerts system, Sentieo ensures you receive all the key news and documents you care about in the fastest and most convenient format possible.

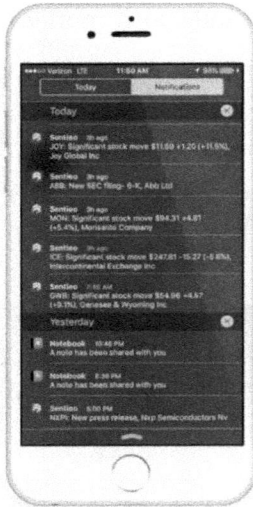

Receive alerts for new documents, new mentions of a search term by companies you follow, major price moves, 52 week highs and lows and inflections in various web data you follow. Receive alerts via email (including full text of documents), alerts within your desktop browser or push notifications to your mobile device.

Mosaic

Use Sentieo's suite of data tracking products to generate Alpha by following a host of real-world consumer, technology, media and telecom related datasets. Sentieo allows you to track, plot and follow thousands of terms to detect inflections in real-time and add a powerful additional piece to your data mosaic.

Sentieo's realtime datasets include: Compete.com, Alexa and SimilarWeb website traffic data, Google Trends searches, Twitter mentions, App downloads and usage.

Call a ticker, keyword or URL to get time-series data and growth rates and quickly compare it to revenue or EBITDA growth. Use the Tracker as a dashboard to look at all the companies you care about and quickly rank order them based on different consumer interest metrics and recent accelerations and decelerations. Use the Plotter's powerful visualization engine to create, save and share complex Plotters tracking all data series you follow for a given ticker.

Example – For Apple (AAPL), follow website traffic, Google searches and quarterly revenue estimates all on the same chart. Easily create a template from Plotter to apply to any other company, share the Plotter with colleagues, and come back months later to view the updated data.

Note – The preceding was an overview of Sentieo, based on Sentieo's marketing brochure provided to me. I have been a happy user of the service, and as mentioned previously, have used data from Sentieo throughout this book. Having used various other competing products such as Factset, ThomsonOne, CapitalIQ, and Bloomberg over the years myself, I can confidently say that Sentieo has broken new ground with its capabilities, and could prove disruptive to high-priced and tech-laggard incumbent competitors. Both the robustness of the datasets and Cloud-based tools provided by Sentieo are not just well designed, but also well thought through from the perspective of research analyst process workflow. Sentieo's integration with OneNote is but one such innovative capability that promise to make the lives of research analysts easier. Other than being a strong supporter of Sentieo's products and believing in their potential, I don't have any direct affiliation with the company itself; nor have I received any monetary reward from Sentieo, beyond their generous provision of data for inclusion in this book.

APPENDIX 3 – Counterpoint Technology Research

General

Counterpoint Research is a young industry analysis and consulting firm, but one that's full of experience. Counterpoint's focus is at the intersection between connected electronics and the ecosystem of software and services enabled by those devices. Their passion is helping their clients make more informed decisions.

Who they are

Counterpoint is a rare thing: a global industry analysis firm headquartered in Asia. Its headquarters are in Hong Kong and its analysts are based in key industry centres globally. Counterpoint has teams based in Seoul, South Korea; Gurgaon and Mumbai, India; London, UK; San Diego, USA; and Buenos Aires, Argentina. Its senior analysts all have industry experience. They've all been in business situations where key strategic and operational decisions had to be made based on the best available information. Too many analyst firms hire people who have had no such experience.

How they started

Counterpoint's founders have worked in management roles in the technology industry for many years. They have also worked as analysts for some of the largest and best known analyst firms.

While in industry, they used the outputs of other analyst firms. In general they found the experience poor in terms of content and frustrating in terms of the business model. When founding Counterpoint, they were determined to create a firm that had a singular purpose – to help clients make better business decisions.

How Counterpoint is different and why it is better

Counterpoint's starting point is wanting to help its clients make better strategic and operational decisions. It employs the most talented people to research and analyse market development. It builds the information assets needed to fully understand the available options. It then packages the information in ways that best suit its clients. And because every client is different, Counterpoint doesn't force you to buy information that is irrelevant. No other analyst firms do this. And every client has access to analyst support so they can ask questions and get guidance on any topic.

Mission

Counterpoint Research provides detailed information and critical insights about the dynamic business environment to help client companies make better strategic and operational decisions. It strives to attract, develop and retain exceptional people.

Vision

The Technology, Media and Telecommunications sector is entering a new epoch in which everything that is powered will compute and everything that computes will be connected. This will generate profound change in the economic, business and social structures around the world. Counterpoint Research will continue to develop its reach and coverage to consistently analyse and quantify the risks and opportunities for clients.

Work Culture

Counterpoint is guided by its vision for how the world of technology is changing, and its mission to help clients positively develop their businesses. The company can only do this by nurturing a team of talented individuals who work with a singular purpose.

Counterpoint has a set of clear values that it applies daily in its pursuit of serving its customers and its team: put clients' interests first; remain independent and impartial; observe the highest ethical standards; use its global reach to deliver the best analysis for all clients; build strong relationships based on trust; maintain an inclusive meritocracy; develop talent through guidance and mentoring.

Note – The preceding was an overview of Counterpoint Technology Research. I have been a happy user of the service, and as mentioned previously, have used data from Counterpoint throughout this book.

Having used various other competing products from providers such as Gartner, IDC, Strategy Analytics, etc. over the years myself, I can confidently say that Counterpoint offers more user-friendly data and services that an investment manager would appreciate. Other than being a strong supporter of Counterpoint's products and services, and believing in their potential, I don't have any direct affiliation with the company itself; nor have I received any monetary reward from Counterpoint, beyond their generous provision of data for inclusion in this book.

APPENDIX 4 – inSpectrum: Semiconductor Industry Intelligence

inSpectrum Tech Inc. is a leading data, research and consulting firm focused on the global technology hardware industry. inSpectrum was founded in 2005, as an independent consultancy to serve not only the largest component suppliers but also the largest buyers, including all major PC, Smartphone, and Tablet OEMs. inSpectrum's independence coupled with its broad view is why it is a trusted source of data and market intelligence in the industry. With a team of analysts and database experts based throughout the globe, inSpectrum is a primary market insight provider to IT professionals, business executives, and the global investment management community.

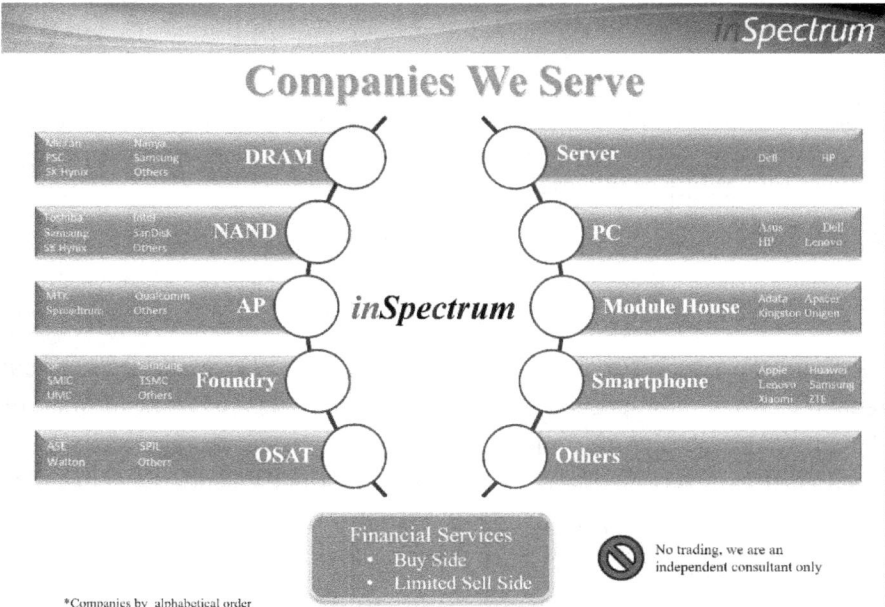

Through primary research and deep industry expertise, inSpectrum analysts are able to forecast market trends in real-time while having a complete view of high-tech vendors' dynamics and future strategy development. inSpectrum offers several products and services through which its clients can take advantage of the insight gained through its research process and time-tested methodologies.

inSpectrum's products & services are designed to provide the most timely and actionable market intelligence on the semiconductor industry. Buyside clients trust inSpectrum's data and insights to help navigate turbulent markets.

Databook - This monthly product summarizes worldwide semiconductor industry data and inSpectrum's proprietary forecasts. The information is clearly organized by company as well as by individual product with separate pages for charts.

Each databook includes: 1) Capacity: Capacity & FAB status by vendor; 2) Output: Organized by month & process; 3) Consumption: Average content by application, Shipments by application, Consumption by application, Unit shipments; 4) ASP & Costs: Sufficiency & price forecasts, Costs by process.

Weekly Reports - This product is sent out at the end of each week and provides clients with the most timely market intelligence. inSpectrum not only highlights important developments but provides analysis of effects on the market. The report highlights: 1) Weekly prices in the spot market; 2) Weekly events affecting the market; 3) Important developments in the semiconductor industry.

Monthly Reports - These reports are produced by inSpectrum's global research team and provide clients with an in-depth view of market dynamics, developments, and their insights. These reports include: 1) Price forecasts & FAB information; 2) Supply WPM and other metrics organized by vendor; 3) Demand drivers organized by product; 4) Easy to read charts.

Presentation - This monthly product provides a clearly articulated summary of inSpectrum's research and findings. With clear analysis and charts, this product is used in many of inSpectrum's meetings and conference calls. It is an added benefit for buyside clients to help interpret inSpectrum's research.

Conference Calls, E-mail Q&A - Conference calls give clients the most up-to-date information on the supply/demand dynamics of the industry as well as insights into individual vendors. These live calls are customized for clients leaving enough time for Q&A. In a separate service, clients may also e-mail inSpectrum a list of questions which inSpectrum answers in Q&A format.

Note – The preceding was an overview of inSpectrum Tech Inc. I have been a happy user of inSpectrum's services, and have found their data to be more reliable, and their services more user-friendly, compared to competitors like DRAMeXchange, Gartner, IDC, and others, particularly in the area of memory semiconductors. Other than being a strong supporter of inSpectrum's products and services, and believing in their potential, I don't have any direct affiliation with the company itself; nor have I received any monetary reward from inSpectrum, beyond their generous provision of data for inclusion in this book.

References

BAJIKAR TECH INVESTOR: http://bajikartechinvestor.com

Vine Street Capital Management, LLC: http://www.vinestreet.net

Jason Zweig's Wall Street Journal articles:
http://topics.wsj.com/person/Z/jason-zweig/1586

Warren Buffet's Berkshire Hathaway investor reports:
http://www.berkshirehathaway.com/reports.html

SumZero Compensation Report: http://www.sumzero.com (buyside access required)

Sentieo: http://sentieo.com

Counterpoint Technology Research: http://counterpointresearch.com

inSpectrum: www.insye.com

Herfindahl-Hirschman Index (HHI):
https://www.justice.gov/atr/herfindahl-hirschman-index

Behavioral Finance Theories and Evidence:
http://www.cfapubs.org/doi/pdf/10.2470/rflr.v3.n1.1

"Window Dressing" for Mutual Funds:
http://www.wsj.com/articles/what-is-window-dressing-for-mutual-funds-1418011555

Glossary

AP – Application Processor

BTS – Wireless Base Station

CAPM – Capital Asset Pricing Model

Cloud – Commonly used to refer to public infrastructure provided through the internet, for accessing email, music, videos, search, and services like file storage and productivity applications

DCF – Discounted Cash Flow

DRAM – Dynamic Random Access Memory – a common type of memory chip used in PCs, Smartphones, Servers, and other electronic devices

DSP – Digital Signal Processor

EOR Switch – End of Rack switch used in data centers to distribute data across multiple racks of servers

ETF – Exchange Traded Fund

EV/S – Enterprise Value to Sales ratio (or multiple)

GAAP – Generally Accepted Accounting Principles

GPS – Global Positioning System

HHI – Herfindahl-Hirschman Index

IC – Integrated circuit Chip

IDM – Integrated Design Manufacturer

IoT – Internet of Things, an ecosystem in which all participating devices are connected to the internet

MNPI – Material Non-Public Information

MPT – Modern Portfolio Theory

NAND – A type of Flash Memory chip commonly used for storing files, music and videos in PCs, Smartphones, Cameras, and other devices

OEM – Original Equipment Manufacturer

OLED – Organic Light Emitting Diode, a type of display that is rapidly growing in popularity

P/B – Price to Book (usually assumed to be Tangible Book Value) ratio or multiple

P/E – Price to Earnings (ratio or multiple)

TOR Switch – Top of Rack switch used to distribute data across multiple servers within a rack

VR/AR – Virtual Reality / Augmented Reality

RADAR – Radio Detection and Ranging

ROIC – Return on Invested Capital

LiDAR – Light Detection and Ranging